MAGNOLIA KITCHEN

MAGNOLIA KITCHEN

Inspired baking with personality

by BERNADETTE GEE

Photography by Lottie Hedley

ALLEN&UNWIN

SYDNEY · MELBOURNE · AUCKLAND · LONDON

business, this has been and continues to be invaluable. I am often asked how to harness social media in marketing, and my answer is always, 'Post lots of cool shit, be authentic and stay true to your own aesthetics and brand.' With that said, I highly recommend that you don't get too caught up in social media—take everything with a grain of salt. Don't compromise who you are for the sake of a couple of empty likes; find value in quality, not quantity.

I continued to stock stores with my fudges, and spent my pregnant life filling orders and creating cakes for auction, which I did once a week as a creative outlet. I really pushed myself during this time, never once slowing down. I recall having a customer come to collect a cake while I was in labour! As soon as the cake was out the door, we hustled into the car and drove straight to the hospital. I was so thankful it was a Thursday because it meant I had five days before I had to prep for my next weekly auction—and yes, five days later and feeling the worse for wear, I still baked all day and did my auction cake as if nothing had changed.

When the customer who won the auction came to collect the cake that week, she asked me 'Weren't you pregnant?'—at which I stepped aside to show a baby asleep on a blanket in the lounge!

By the time Edward was six months old, things had really started to heat up with Magnolia Kitchen's social media presence. Our humble little Instagram was really taking hold and I had taken to Snapchat as a way of keeping myself sane, sharing all aspects of my life as a mum and business owner trying to juggle babies, family and work all at once. It was very lonely being in a kitchen by myself, and social media was my virtual therapist's couch. I got to talk about my issues honestly, with mostly no judgement, and I gradually built up a community of like-minded followers around the world who listened to me, laughed with me, watched my business grow and supported me. It was this platform I turned to that fateful day in June 2016 when my business came crashing down around me.

When I was heavily pregnant with Edward I had made the decision to reduce the number of orders I was doing, and therefore didn't see the need to keep hiring a commercial kitchen—knowing that after we'd had Edward we would start hunting for a premises where we could set up shop properly. Unfortunately, a 'concerned citizen' decided to contact the local council and have us shut down for producing from a home kitchen without a licence. I have never felt so distraught in my *life*. I was forced to cancel all existing orders, and stopped supplying all of my stockists. I was heartbroken that someone had taken such a harsh step towards destroying my business.

As soon as I received the call to cease and desist, I took to social media, tears and all, to share my pain with my community. I will never forget the flood of support I received that day from complete strangers; it was truly heartwarming. My friends and family rallied around, and not being one to cry into my pillow for too long, I picked myself up. Determined not to throw away what I had worked so hard for, I sprang into action.

I realised that Magnolia Kitchen's products were not all that the business had to offer; it occurred to me that I, personally, was a bankable commodity. The cake skills I had developed over the years—the skills that had exploded my social media worldwide—actually counted for something. Not only that, but I suddenly had an abundance of free time on my hands: a chance to step back and really focus on the business.

With my new determination to show the world that it takes more than that to stop me, I threw myself into finding a premises for Magnolia Kitchen. We eventually settled on a spot in Silverdale village. The most common thing we heard was 'Why Silverdale?' and 'You won't have enough foot traffic.' What *I* knew that no one else did, however, was that Magnolia Kitchen Sweet Cafe would be a destination and would draw in the crowds based on our already strong following. While our local following was still small, I knew I could woo people with amazing sweet treats and consistently good coffee.

We signed the lease in early August 2016 and were lucky enough to take over the premises a couple of weeks early. Harley and I got stuck into the fit-out. Of course we had zero experience in what it took to fit out a commercial kitchen and cafe, but with the help of friends and family— specifically my daughter's family, who were so generous with their building skills, time and effort—we made it happen.

It was a manic time juggling the two boys, with Harley working full-time, and of course the fact that our wedding was fast approaching on 1 October and required a whole lot of planning. Charlotte was an amazing babysitter and spent many nights with her brothers while Harley and I slaved away into the wee hours sanding and painting, etc. Harley, bless him, planned our entire wedding; he would run details past me while I focused on the fit-out and on securing vendors and equipment. Where the wedding was concerned, I was responsible for my and my bridesmaids' dresses and showing up on the day. We made the decision to open the cafe officially after our wedding, although as soon as the coffee machine was installed I wasn't turning away customers.

Harley did an exemplary job and our wedding was amazingly beautiful—one of the happiest days of my life. We said our *I do*'s and enjoyed an incredible

OPPOSITE (CLOCKWISE FROM TOP LEFT) The necklace says it all; my carrot cake recipe made as a loaf and iced with lemon white chocolate ganache; the cabinet at Magnolia Kitchen; staff member Sam decorating a unicorn horn while Sarah ices a cake.

day and night with our nearest and dearest. The next day we promptly hopped on a plane to Samoa, leaving the kids, Magnolia Kitchen and real life behind, and immersed ourselves in our honeymoon as newlyweds.

We arrived back in New Zealand relaxed and refreshed on 9 October 2016; the next day, a Monday, Magnolia Kitchen Sweet Cafe officially opened its doors. We had a small opening party that week to celebrate. I was overwhelmed by what I had achieved. I kept looking around and thinking, *Is this real?* Of course, the stress and hard work was yet to begin—opening the doors was only the first step. Working hard day in, day out to keep them open became my focus.

I opened Magnolia Kitchen Sweet Cafe with just one staff member: *me*. It would be another six weeks before I took on my first employee. Those first six weeks were *insane*. I would be at the shop from 5 a.m., baking and juggling the front of house, making coffees and serving customers. I look back at this time and don't know how I survived— though of course I know that I survived because I am stubborn as fuck and because I have the most amazing support system. My husband, my family, my friends and my ever-growing online and local community are the reason that Magnolia Kitchen exists.

To have that many people supporting your dream is overwhelming and heartwarming all at once. Building a business and a brand out of passion has been so rewarding. Our journey has been filled with its fair share of drama and I feel that I'm on a rollercoaster most days. Thankfully the highs outweigh the lows, and I am truly blessed to be living my dream.

The year 2018 has seen Magnolia Kitchen expand and take over the premises next door to the Sweet Cafe, which is now a full commercial kitchen used for wholesale production of our retail products that we distribute to about 20 boutique food stores and gift shops around New Zealand. We have launched worldwide shipping through our online shop, and are thrilled to be growing our merchandise range and to have people eating our treats and using our tools worldwide.

Today, we have huge plans for Magnolia Kitchen, and thanks to my amazing staff I am able to work on these plans and make our brand all I know it can be, and more. Magnolia Kitchen Sweet Cafe is a true destination in its own right: it keeps the local community fuelled on sugar and caffeine, and brings crowds from all around New Zealand. We are even lucky enough to have our fair share of international visitors.

I can't thank our customers, followers and community (online and local) enough for their continued support of Magnolia Kitchen and myself.

OPPOSITE Art or cake? Handpainted by Bets; design inspired by a mural on the wall of R & D Kitchen in Grey Lynn.

To my family and friends who have given so much of themselves to my dream, your support is unwavering and so very much appreciated. Without you all standing behind me and alongside me, I would never have been able to achieve the great things I have thus far. I will never forget each and every one of your efforts and I LOVE you all from the bottom of my heart. THANK YOU.

I would also like to say a few things to the most special individuals in my life. I have attempted to write this so many times, and I am such a sook that I keep crying and can't get started! At this point I am three weeks past my extended deadline and I'm pretty sure I'll be in trouble with my publisher if I don't get it done. So here goes nothing—tears and all.

HARLEY

I think I could probably write an entire book on how grateful I am to this man. Whenever I am asked, 'How do you manage to raise three kids, and run a home *and* a business?', my response is always, 'I have an amazing husband.' This couldn't be more true. Harley is the most supportive, tolerant, loving, kind person I have ever met and I am beyond lucky to have this guy in my corner each and every day. Not only does he work extremely hard at his own job, he is also there every night picking up the kids from daycare, coming home and cooking dinner, bathing the kids and running bedtime. He is also my number-one supporter, always there to pick me up after my whirlwind tantrums and meltdowns over how hard life is or how someone was mean to me online, or giving me pep talks when I am freaking out that I have no idea what I'm doing. He's often on the receiving end of my moods and still manages to love me through it all. He tells me I am an amazing mum when I feel less than amazing. His unwavering support for me and my dream is something to be applauded. Harley, you are and always will be my forever—without your love and support I wouldn't be where I am today. You are an incredible person, dad and husband, and I can't thank you enough for everything you contribute to my and the kids' lives. Thank you for being my team. xx

CHARLOTTE

You, my darling daughter, are just as much Magnolia Kitchen as I am. You have been my number one for over 16 years now and I couldn't have asked for a better daughter to join me on this parenting journey. You have been there for me through everything, and no matter what I do you always have my back. You are an amazing human and have grown into a smart and talented woman who I am so ridiculously proud of. Thank you for being you, for supporting me, and for all your hard work helping out in those early days of Magnolia Kitchen, packing fudge and labelling boxes. You are now a Magnolia Kitchen employee

OPPOSITE (CLOCKWISE FROM TOP LEFT)
Edwardo, Destroyer of Worlds; my girl Charlotte, my confidante and my pride; Jamesy Gee, the face of mischief.

DOUGHS
& LOAVES

—

BASIC BRIOCHE DOUGH

TIMING

PREP 20 mins

PROOFING approx.
3 hours, or overnight

MAKES approx. 700 g

INGREDIENTS
2 eggs
50 g (1¾ oz) caster sugar
1 tablespoon salt
240 ml (8 fl oz) milk
10 g (¼ oz) instant dry yeast
170 g (6 oz) butter
560 g (1 lb 4¼ oz) flour

This dough can be made into a brioche scroll, doughnuts, fruit loaf or hot cross buns. There's not a day that goes by when you won't thank your bloody stars for this recipe—it is so versatile and will become a staple in your kitchen. I encourage you all to get inspired and see what sweet delights you can create (and savoury, but don't tell sweet I said that because that is grounds for divorce).

METHOD

In your mixer bowl, whisk together the eggs, sugar and salt.

Pour the milk into a suitable bowl, and heat in your microwave (in short bursts) until lukewarm*. Now add your yeast to the lukewarm milk and whisk to combine. Add the milk and yeast mixture to your mixer bowl and stir to combine.

Use the same bowl you used for the milk to melt your butter in the microwave—this will save on dishes (you're welcome). Add the melted butter to your mixer bowl and mix to combine. Add half the quantity of flour and whisk by hand to combine.

Now put the dough-hook attachment on your mixer and add the remaining flour to the bowl. Mix on low speed until the flour is combined, then increase to medium speed and leave mixing for about 5 mins. The dough will start to climb up on the dough hook and pull away from the sides of the mixer bowl. (This is one of those instructions where you will just have to trust me—and you will be like 'A-ha!' when you see it climbing the hook.)

If you're making this dough for hot cross buns or fruit loaf, now is the time to add the spices, zest and dried fruit. Continue to knead for a further 2 mins until combined.

Transfer the dough to the same bowl you melted the butter in (saving on dishes again!). Cover the dough with plastic wrap, pressing the wrap gently against the dough. Place in the fridge and proof for about 3 hours (or you can leave it overnight).

* I know recipes often say 'lukewarm' but what is lukewarm? Who is Luke? This is really random, so I'm gonna try to describe what lukewarm is. Put your finger in your mouth now. Hopefully your mouth is warm—this is my best description of lukewarm.

MACADAMIA, WHITE CHOCOLATE & SALTED CARAMEL BRIOCHE SCROLLS

TIMING

PREP 8 mins (with your dough and filling already prepped)

PROOFING 30–60 mins

BAKING approx. 45 mins

MAKES 8 pieces

INGREDIENTS

1 recipe Basic Brioche Dough (page 31)

1 recipe Almond Filling (overleaf)

150 g (5½ oz) chopped macadamias

150 g (5½ oz) white chocolate buttons

100 g (3½ oz) Salted Caramel (page 129), to drizzle

icing sugar, to dust

My love affair with brioche began one summer's day back in the mid-2000s when I took a second job on Saturdays to make some extra cash. At this point I had a toddler and was raising her solo while in the Navy, so the extra cash was needed—and, if I'm honest, I bloody loved cooking and baking and the social banter that comes when working in a kitchen. I took a job as breakfast cook at a local cafe where my sister worked (I think she vouched for me—thanks little sis!), and they served brioche scrolls every day. These things were drool-worthy, and I always used to hope like fuck there'd be one left over at the end of my shift. Since then I've had brioche as part of my repertoire, always striving for that drool-worthy brioche scroll from back in the day. When I opened the doors of Magnolia Kitchen Sweet Cafe, guess what? Brioche was absolutely the first thing on the menu. Side note: who among my social media following remembers my 5 a.m. starts when I used to Snapchat myself making the brioche every day?

METHOD

Prep a 23 cm (9 in) round baking tin with cooking spray and a lining of baking paper. Remove the dough from the fridge, place it on a benchtop dusted with flour and knead it slightly until it's smooth.

Using a rolling pin, roll the dough into a rough rectangle about 10 cm wide and 40 cm long. Spread the Almond Filling evenly over all of the dough and sprinkle the macadamias and white chocolate over that, making sure everything is evenly spread.

Starting at one of the long ends, roll the dough up into a sausage. Cut your sausage into pieces about 5 cm (2 in) long, placing each piece in the tin with a cut side up so you can see the scroll. Make sure the scrolls are close together, with just a 1 cm (½ in) gap between them to allow for rising. Cover with plastic wrap and allow to proof somewhere until risen and puffy (this can take up to an hour).

Continued overleaf

Preheat your oven to 160°C (315°F). Remove the plastic wrap and put the scrolls in the oven with a baking tray sitting on top of the tin. Allow to bake for at least 20 mins with the tray on top, then remove the tray to allow the brioche to brown up during the remaining 25 mins or so.

Test the brioche with a knife—stick it in between the scrolls and give it a wriggle from side to side. If the knife comes out clean, you're good to go; if it comes out doughy, well then keep on baking for a bit longer.

When it's done, allow to cool in the tin for a bit, then turn out onto a wire rack to cool further. Dust with icing sugar and drizzle with a generous amount of salted caramel. Eat while warm for the most enjoyable eating experience.

ALMOND FILLING

TIMING
PREP 10 mins
MAKES approx. 400 g

100 g (3½ oz) almond meal
100 g (3½ oz) butter, melted
1 tablespoon ground cinnamon
200 g (7 oz) brown sugar

METHOD
Put all ingredients* together in a bowl and mix well to form a paste.
THE END.

* For an allergy-friendly version, replace the melted butter with a dairy-free spread (I use Olivani).

FLAVOUR INSPO FOR BRIOCHE SCROLLS

——

Here are some more flavour ideas to get you started. I always encourage creativity so don't be afraid to mix it up.

RASPBERRY DARK CHOCOLATE
Replace the macadamias and white chocolate with 150 g (5½ oz) frozen raspberries and 150 g (5½ oz) chopped dark chocolate.

MAPLE & PECAN
Replace the macadamias and white chocolate with 150 g (5½ oz) pecans, and drizzle with 100 g (3½ oz) maple syrup instead of the salted caramel.

ORANGE DARK CHOCOLATE
Replace the macadamias and white chocolate with the zest of 1 orange and 150 g (5½ oz) chopped dark chocolate.

MANGO & COCONUT
Replace the macadamias and white chocolate with 150 g (5½ oz) frozen diced mango and 150 g (5½ oz) desiccated coconut.

PEACH & WHITE CHOCOLATE
Replace the macadamias with 150 g (5½ oz) drained canned peaches (keep the white chocolate buttons!).

METHOD

Warm your coconut milk and dairy-free butter in a suitable bowl in your microwave until just warmed and the butter is starting to melt. DO NOT OVERHEAT IT or you will fuck it up and probs blame me. Consider this your warning.

Put the aquafaba*, sugar and salt in your mixer bowl, bung the whisk attachment on and whip until you get stiff peaks. This shit will blow your mind.

Sprinkle the yeast over the warm coconut milk mixture and mix to combine. Add this mixture to the whipped aquafaba along with the flour and guar gum. Switch to the paddle attachment and mix on low speed for about 8 mins, until well mixed into a dough.

If you're making this dough for hot cross buns or fruit loaf, add the spices, zest and dried fruit listed in those recipes now. Continue to knead for a further 2 mins until combined. Transfer the dough to a greased container and cover with plastic wrap. Place the container somewhere warm to allow the dough to proof. You want it to double in size and get big air bubbles through it; at that point, transfer the container to the fridge for about 3 hours.

While your dough is chilling the fuck out, you can decide what you are going to do with it—brioche scrolls, hot cross buns, fruit loaf or doughnuts (see recipes on the following pages). Please be aware that this dough is sticky and a bit different to normal dough. I've found that rolling it between two sheets of plastic wrap rather than adding extra flour works best.

* Check out my story about this stuff near the top of page 26.

ALLERGY-FRIENDLY BRIOCHE SCROLLS

TIMING

PREP 8 mins (once your dough is made)

PROOFING 30–60 mins

BAKING approx. 45 mins

MAKES 8 pieces

INGREDIENTS

1 recipe Allergy-friendly Basic Brioche Dough (page 44)

1 recipe allergy-friendly Almond Filling (page 34)

100 g (3½ oz) chopped frozen fruit or nuts

100 g (3½ oz) allergy-friendly chocolate

Allergy-friendly Salted Caramel (page 131), to drizzle

icing sugar, to dust

METHOD

Prep a 20 cm (8 in) round baking tin with cooking spray and line the bottom with baking paper. Spread a good layer of plastic wrap over your workbench. Remove your pre-made dough from the fridge, put it on top of the plastic wrap and gently form it into a sausage. *snigger*

Place more plastic wrap on top of the dough—this makes it less of a sticky mess to roll out. Using a rolling pin (if you don't have one, I've been known to have great rolling success with a wine bottle), roll the dough into a rough rectangle about 10 cm (4 in) wide and 40 cm (16 in) long. Remove the plastic wrap from the top. Spread your almond filling over the whole of the dough—be gentle, as you can easily tear the dough doing this. Sprinkle the fruit or nuts (another *snigger*) and the chocolate evenly over the top.

Using the plastic wrap underneath the dough, take one of the long ends and fold the edge of the dough onto itself, then continue to use the plastic wrap to roll the dough up into another sausage—but DON'T roll the plastic wrap into it! Now CUT THE dough SAUSAGE into pieces about 5 cm (2 in) long, placing each piece in the tin with a cut side up so you can see the scroll. Make sure the scrolls are close together with just a 1 cm (½ in) gap between them to allow for rising. Cover with plastic wrap and allow to proof in a warm place until risen and puffy. This can take up to an hour.

Preheat your oven to 160°C (315°F). Remove the plastic wrap and put the tin in the oven with a baking tray sitting on top of it. Allow to bake for at least 20 mins with the tray on top, then remove the tray to allow the brioche to brown up while it bakes for about another 25 mins.

Test the brioche with a knife—stick it between your scrolls and give it a wriggle from side to side. If the knife comes out clean, you fucken did it—well done. If the knife comes out doughy, just keep baking a bit longer.

When it's cooked, allow to cool in the tin for a bit, then turn out onto a wire rack to cool further. Drizzle with Allergy-friendly Salted Caramel and dust with icing sugar. Eat while warm and rejoice in the almighty Bets (and Bruce of aquafaba fame, 'cause ya know he is the Messiah).

ALLERGY-FRIENDLY BRIOCHE DOUGHNUTS

FREE FROM GLUTEN, EGGS, DAIRY AND ANIMAL PRODUCTS

TIMING

PREP 15 mins (once you've made the dough)

PROOFING 1 hour

FRYING approx. 30 mins

MAKES 8 doughnuts

INGREDIENTS

1 recipe Allergy-friendly Basic Brioche Dough (page 44)

800 ml (28 fl oz) canola oil

250 g (9 oz) caster sugar

20 g (¾ oz) ground cinnamon

Raise your hand if you're fizzing at the bung at the thought of an allergy-friendly doughnut in yo' mouth. Because ya know you have them allergies and therefore doughnuts are like a delicious teasing delight that would usually mean PAIN, ILLNESS AND NOTHING GOOD if ingested.

METHOD

Remove that chilled-as dough from the fridge, grease your hands with a little cooking oil and give the dough a little knead to make sure it's smooth. Roll it out between two pieces of plastic wrap until about 3 cm (1¼ in) thick. Using a round cookie cutter about 8 cm (3¼ in) across, cut out as many doughnuts as you can. Knead the off-cuts back together and do some more rolling and cutting. You can leave your doughnuts whole or you can cut holes in the centre using the big end of a piping nozzle to get classic-style doughnuts.

Place the doughnuts on a tray, cover with plastic wrap and allow to proof in a warm place for an hour.

When the doughnuts are nearly risen, pour the oil into a deep pot and heat it to 170°C (325°F). Once the oil has reached that temperature, gently place a few doughnuts in the hot oil, being careful not to overcrowd the pot. Set a timer for 3½ mins. When it bleeps, flip the doughnuts over and re-start the timer for an additional 3½ mins. Test to see if they're done by giving them a poke with a skewer or metal knitting needle. If it comes out clean, they're ready and you can use your tongs to remove them from the oil onto some paper towels.

While the doughnuts are frying, mix together the sugar and cinnamon. Once each batch has been fried, roll the doughnuts in the cinnamon sugar.

If you have left your doughnuts whole, you can now use an apple corer to make a hole two-thirds of the way into the doughnut and fill it with jam or anything else you like. Have a look through the curds and fillings in the book (pages 103–139)—I'm sure you'll find inspo.

ALLERGY-FRIENDLY HOT CROSS BRIOCHE BUNS

TIMING

PREP 8 mins (plus dough making)

PROOFING 30–60 mins

BAKING 30–40 mins

MAKES 9 buns

INGREDIENTS

Buns

1 recipe Allergy-friendly Basic Brioche Dough with the following spice, zest and dried fruit* added (when instructed in the recipe page 44)

2 tablespoons mixed spice

zest of 1 orange

80 g (2¾ oz) sultanas

80 g (2¾ oz) raisins

Crosses

30 g (1 oz) warm water

100 g (3½ oz) gluten-free plain flour

Glaze

100 g (3½ oz) caster sugar

¼ teaspoon vanilla bean paste

50 ml (1½ fl oz) boiling water

METHOD

Prep a deepish 20 cm (8 in) square baking tin with cooking spray and line the bottom with baking paper.

Spread a little neutral-flavoured oil over your benchtop. Remove your dough from the fridge and knead it on the benchtop a few times until smooth. Cut the dough into nine evenly sized pieces—use your scales to weigh them to make sure they're all the same. Make a cage with your fingers around each of the pieces of dough in turn, and move your hand in a circular motion so that your fingertips are just touching the bottom of the dough—this should give you a nice evenly round bun.

Place the buns in the tin so that they are just touching. Cover with plastic wrap and allow to proof for about an hour in a warm area, until doubled in size.

Meanwhile, prepare the cross mix by adding small amounts of the water to the gluten-free flour and mixing in well. The paste should be nice and smooth, and you want it to be a slightly runny piping consistency. When it looks right, put the cross mix in a piping bag and snip off the end about 3 mm (⅛ in) from the bottom.

Preheat your oven to 160°C (315°F). Pipe crosses onto your risen buns and bake them for 30–40 mins until they're golden and a knife comes out clean when you stab it into them.

Prepare the glaze by dissolving the sugar and vanilla bean paste in the boiling water. When the buns are ready, take them out of the oven and brush them with glaze immediately while they're still in the tin. After a few mins cooling, move them to a wire rack.

Serve warm with a dairy-free butter substitute.

* For a chocolate version, sub the dried fruit for 150 g (5½ oz) dairy-free chocolate chips.

ALLERGY-FRIENDLY BRIOCHE FRUIT LOAF

FREE FROM GLUTEN, EGGS, DAIRY AND ANIMAL PRODUCTS

TIMING

PREP 8 mins (plus dough making)

PROOFING approx. 1 hour

BAKING approx. 50 mins

MAKES 1 standard loaf

INGREDIENTS

1 recipe Allergy-friendly Basic Brioche Dough with the following spice, zest and dried fruit added (when instructed in the recipe page 44)

2 tablespoons mixed spice

zest of 1 orange

80 g (2¾ oz) sultanas

80 g (2¾ oz) raisins

Glaze

100 g (3½ oz) caster sugar

¼ teaspoon vanilla bean paste

50 ml (1½ fl oz) boiling water

METHOD

Prepare a loaf tin with cooking spray.

Spread a little neutral-flavoured oil on your benchtop. Take your dough out of the fridge and knead it slightly until smooth, then form it into a fat sausage shape. Place your hands on either side of the sausage and just above it, then pull the dough surface down and fold it under. This will give your dough a nice smooth top.

Place your dough sausage in your tin, cover it with plastic wrap and leave it in a warm place for an hour to proof. Just before it's ready, preheat your oven to 160°C (315°F).

Put your loaf in the oven and bake for about 50 mins or until a knife stabbed into it comes out clean. Give the knife a wiggle when it's in the loaf; if it isn't cooked properly, the dough will stick to the knife.

Prepare the glaze by dissolving the sugar and vanilla bean paste in the boiling water. When the loaf comes out of the oven, brush it with glaze immediately while still in the tin. Allow it to cool slightly on a wire rack before slicing and spreading with a dairy-free butter substitute.

Slices of unbuttered brioche loaf can be stored in the freezer (lay pieces of baking paper between the slices to stop them sticking together). When you're in need of a quick breakfast or snack, pop a slice straight into your toaster and then butter it—awesome doesn't get much quicker than this.

MAGNOLIA KITCHEN SIGNATURE RICH CHOCOLATE CAKE

TIMING

PREP 20 mins

BAKING 30–40 mins

CHILLING 2 hours

MAKES 3 x 18 cm (7 in) round layers

SERVES approx. 18 when decorated

INGREDIENTS

365 g (12¾ oz) plain flour

600 g (1 lb 5 oz) brown sugar

120 g (4½ oz) Dutch cocoa

15 g (½ oz) baking soda

250 g (9 oz) butter, at room temperature

1 teaspoon instant coffee (or 30 g [1 oz] shot of espresso)

370 g (12½ oz) warm water

4 whole eggs

120 g (4¼ oz) canola oil

2 teaspoons vanilla extract

260 g (9¼ oz) buttermilk

OPPOSITE See pages 119–121 for how to achieve the mirror glaze design shown on this rich chocolate cake.

You need to know that this is the BEST chocolate cake EVER—it is my signature recipe, and to date only my staff and my sister know it. It keeps everyone happy, even the 'I don't like chocolate cake' people out there (you know who you are). It is rich and chocolatey, but at the same time light in texture. It has served me well for so many years and was the first cake I sold for money way back when. I might even go so far as to say that the feedback on the deliciousness of this cake from that very first sale is what gave me the confidence to become Magnolia Kitchen. It will continue to serve me well for years to come, and now that I am sharing it with you guys I know it will serve you well too.

METHOD

Preheat your oven to 170°C (325°F). Prepare three 18 cm (7 in) cake tins with cooking spray or butter and line with baking paper.

Place the flour, sugar, cocoa and baking soda in the bowl of a stand mixer fitted with the paddle attachment, and mix on low to combine. Add the butter and mix on low until the mixture resembles breadcrumbs. (You could do this by hand—see the vanilla cake recipe on page 61—but really, the stand mixer is the way to go.)

In a separate bowl, dissolve the instant coffee in the warm water (or just use the shot of espresso), add the eggs, oil and vanilla and mix together. Add two-thirds of the wet mixture to the dry ingredients and mix on medium-high until thick and fluffy. Add the remaining wet ingredients and mix well until combined and the batter is smooth. Make sure you scrape down the bowl and then continue mixing, as the dry mixture can get stuck at the bottom and you really want a nice, smooth consistency.

Add the buttermilk and mix slowly to combine. There may be small chunks of buttermilk but don't fret, this is normal. This batter is also wetter than the basic vanilla recipe, so don't panic if it's not thick.

Continued overleaf

Pour the mixture evenly into the prepared tins (use your scales to get them all the same; see my tips on page 25), and bake for 30–40 mins until a skewer or knitting needle poked into the cakes comes out clean. Allow to cool in the tins for 5–10 mins, then turn out onto cooling racks.

When the cakes are cool, wrap them in plastic wrap and chill for 2 hours or overnight—this will make them easier to trim and ice (see my instructional on this, pages 68–79).

This cake goes perfectly with EVERY type of icing. If you are after something classic, go for Dark Chocolate Ganache (page 115); if you want to balance the rich chocolate cake with something lighter, use Vanilla Bean Swiss Meringue Buttercream (page 107).

You can also add coconut or frozen fruit to this cake to change up the chocolatey flavour profile. See our flavour inspos below for . . . well, inspo of course.

FLAVOUR INSPO FOR CHOCOLATE CAKE

Try out these flavour variations with my rich chocolate cake recipe.

ORANGE CHOCOLATE CAKE
Replace the vanilla extract in the wet ingredients with 1 teaspoon of orange oil (LorAnn).

BERRY CHOCOLATE CAKE
Make the cake as per the recipe, then distribute 180 g (6 oz) frozen berries evenly over the batter and bake as normal. If using larger berries such as strawberries or boysenberries, chop these up before adding to the batter.

COCONUT CHOCOLATE CAKE
Add 150 g (5½ oz) desiccated coconut to the dry ingredients at the start.

CAKE ASSEMBLY & ICING INSTRUCTIONAL

YOU WILL NEED

3 chilled one-layer cakes, plus icing (and filling, if using)

ruler

large serrated knife or cake trimmer tool

masonite board

2 cake cards

double-sided tape

cake turntable

offset spatula

piping bag

sharp-as-shit scraper

regular spatula

cake detailing palette knife

Here are my all-important secret tips and tricks for beautiful three-layer cakes—I can't tell you what a weight off my shoulders it is to finally share these! (The next instructional tells you how to create my two-tier cakes, once you've layered up and iced two three-layer cakes.)

TRIMMING

Before you begin, gather all your tools. Remove your cakes from the fridge and unwrap.

1. Hold your ruler vertically to measure the height of each cake, and mark where you are going to trim. Make a note of this measurement and use it for all of your layers.

2. Trim the top off each cake so they are flat. If you don't have a cake trimmer tool, I recommend using a large serrated knife.

3. Remove the trimmed tops and set aside; these offcuts can be kept for snacks or used for making cake pops.

4. Once you have levelled each layer, stack them on top of each other, and use your serrated knife to trim all the way around, removing about 2 mm (¹⁄₁₆ in) of cake. This will leave room between the cake and the edge of the board for the icing.

BOARD PREP

As the base for my standard buttercream or ganache cakes, I use a masonite board plus a 1 mm (1/32 in) cake card. The cake cards are the same size as the cake—so if the tins you baked the cakes in are 18 cm (7 in), then you need two 18 cm (7 in) cake cards. You then use a larger masonite base board, for example a 20 cm (8 in) board.

Using double-sided sticky tape, attach one of the cake cards to the base board with the silver side facing up. Make sure that the cake card is totally central on top of the board—this is your guide for those sharp-as-shit smooth edges. Place the prepped board on the turntable. Set aside the remaining cake card—you'll use this later when icing the cake.

ICING THE CAKE

1. Prep your icing. If you're using buttercream, make sure it is whipped and soft; if you're using ganache, make sure it is softened to a spreadable consistency. Using your offset spatula, smear a blob of icing on the cake card.

2. Gently place your first layer of cake on the cake card—make sure it is bang in the centre and there is a gap between the edge of the cake and the edge of the card. If the cake is too close to the edge of the card, your cake will show through when you ice it (semi-naked style).

3. Scoop a generous amount of icing onto the top of the cake and spread evenly with your offset spatula. If you are just icing the cake without additional fillings, skip to step 6.

4. Put some of your icing into a piping bag without a nozzle, and cut about 1.5 cm (5/8 in) off the bottom of the bag. Now pipe a line of icing around the edge of the cake—this will act like a dam to ensure no filling leaks out.

Continued overleaf

5. Add your filling and spread it evenly inside the dam wall.

6. Carefully add the second layer of cake, making sure it is centred and aligned. Press it down firmly.

7. Spread a small amount of icing around the first two layers to lock in the crumbs—this is called a crumb coating. Move your offset spatula back and forth, pushing the icing into the cake, and scrape away any excess crumb-filled icing.

8. Repeat steps 3–7 to add your third layer of cake, making sure all the layers are aligned and level.

9. Scoop a generous amount of icing on top of the third layer and spread it evenly with your offset spatula.

10. Place the second cake card, silver side down, centrally on top of the icing.

11. Hold your sharp-as-shit scraper against both cake cards, top and bottom—you want the scraper to be completely parallel.

12. Once you are satisfied that the top cake card is parallel to the bottom one, start adding icing. Using your regular spatula, scrape generous amounts of icing onto the side of the cake, using the top cake board to scrape the icing off the spatula.

13. Completely cover the cake, ensuring that your messy-as-fuck icing extends past both cake cards.

Continued overleaf

16

14. Now for the fun part: grab your sharp-as-shit scraper and hold it at about a 60-degree angle with the edge flush against the icing but not yet touching the cake cards. While pulling the scraper towards you, turn the turntable—you want to gently scrape back the icing in quarter-turns until you have removed 80% of the excess icing. Position the scraper, do a quarter-turn, remove the icing from the scraper, wipe clean, and repeat. For the last 20%, you want to use a full rotation of the turntable with every scrape—no stopping and starting, people, it's a FULL ROTATION.

15. If you find along the way that you haven't put enough excess icing on the cake and you have icing craters, or there's a spot that isn't quite as perfect as you'd like, you can go back in using your offset spatula. Add excess icing to the spot you want to fix, but also add icing above and below it so that the excess is fully spread from top card to bottom card.

16. Repeat your scraping in full rotations until perfection is achieved. Move your cake to the fridge and chill it for about 1 hour.

17. Once chilled, gently pull up the edge of the top cake card—it should pull straight off, revealing a perfect sharp-as-shit edge. If some icing comes away when you pull the card off, don't worry—everything is fixable. Just use your cake detailing palette knife to replace any icing that has pulled off and smooth it flat. The cake is already cold, so this icing should set straight away.

18. To tidy up the top of the cake, use your cake detailing palette knife at a 45-degree angle pointing up towards you and gently scrape back the rough icing. Be particularly careful around the edges. You really want to be only just scraping with the palette knife, not putting any real pressure on.

19. This is what a perfect sharp-as-shit edge looks like.

19

DECORATING THE CAKE

1. To decorate in the abstract oil paint style I'm showing you here, put a dollop of your plain, uncoloured icing on one of your sharp-as-shit scrapers (these double as an artist's palette), keeping the rest off to one side. Choose a colour and mix it with the icing on the scraper to get the darkest shade you want. Start adding this dark-coloured icing to your cake, using a swishing motion as if you are painting but with a palette knife.

2. Keep a diagonal motion going up and around the cake, and as you go start to add some of the uncoloured icing to your palate. This will mix with the darker colour and you will achieve an abstract ombre oil paint effect.

3. When you are satisfied with the amount of icing you have added, place some dried rose petals among the oil-painted effect to add another dimension.

STORAGE

Store buttercream cakes in the fridge; for ganache, leave at room temperature as long as it is a cool room with no direct sunlight.

RED VELVET
MINI CAKES

TIMING

PREP 20 mins

BAKING approx.
15 mins

MAKES 12 mini cakes

INGREDIENTS

150 g (5½ oz) plain
flour

150 g (5½ oz) caster
sugar

30 g (1 oz) cocoa
powder

65 g (2¼ oz) butter,
at room temperature

120 g (4¼ oz)
buttermilk

1 egg

½ teaspoon red gel
food colour

2 teaspoons cider
vinegar

1 teaspoon baking
soda

To decorate

500 g (1 lb 2 oz)
Vanilla Bean Cream
Cheese Icing
(page 112)

Red velvet cake always perplexed me . . . I was always being asked 'What's red velvet cake?' and I never knew how to answer. So I went away and researched, but couldn't really find much solid info on how it originated. Today I tell people it is a delicious velvet crumb cake with underlying cocoa notes. Not as chocolate-rich as chocolate cake, but not as chocolate-free as vanilla cake. The red, well, who bloody knows, but should we really argue? To me, the red makes this cake a perfect deep burgundy colour rather than the weak brown it would no doubt be without it. However this cake happened to be, I'll tell you this—it's delicious and pairs perfectly with Vanilla Bean Cream Cheese Icing (page 112).

You can also make this as a layer cake. This recipe will make a single 18-cm (7-in) cake, so if you want your cake to have three layers—which is the standard Magnolia Kitchen style—then multiply the recipe by three.

METHOD

Preheat your oven to 180°C (350°F). Prep a square mini cake tray with baking spray (I use a silicone one that is like a muffin tray but square—or you could make them round if you wanted).

Place the flour, sugar and cocoa in the bowl of your stand mixer fitted with the paddle attachment, and mix on LOW to combine. (Note that if you accidentally put it on high you'll end up with a face full of flour and cocoa, and will likely be picking cocoa out of your nose for the rest of the day.) Chop your butter into cubes, add it to the dry ingredients and mix on low until the mixture resembles breadcrumbs. (You can do this by hand, as I've explained in the vanilla bean cake recipe on page 61, but seriously, use a stand mixer!)

In a separate bowl, mix together the buttermilk, egg and food colour—don't forget to *oooh* and *ahhhh* at the pretty colour. Add two-thirds of the buttermilk mixture to the mixer bowl, and mix on medium-high until combined. Add the remaining buttermilk mixture and mix well until combined and the batter is fluffy and a light burgundy colour.

Continued overleaf

Combine the cider vinegar and baking soda—just like in science class, this will bubble up. Add your bubbly soda to the batter and mix on low to combine. Scoop the mixture evenly into the prepared tray and bake for about 15 mins, until a skewer comes out clean when pokey-poked into the cakes. Allow to cool in the tin for 5–10 mins, then turn out onto cooling racks.

Once your mini cakes are cooled, trim any domes off the top with a serrated knife so that the surface is flat. Reserve your off-cuts for later.

Prep a piping bag with a suitable nozzle (I use an Ateco size 855), and fill it with your cream cheese icing. Pipe a swirl of icing on top of each mini cake and finish with a sprinkle of crumbled-up off-cuts for a nice burgundy accent.

ICING SUGGESTIONS

If you are making mini cakes or a simple layer cake, then ice with the suggested cream cheese icing. If you plan on decorating the cake once iced, then I recommend a Vanilla Bean White Chocolate Ganache (page 117) with cream cheese flavour. The ganache will provide added structure and allow the cake to be stored at room temperature.

OPPOSITE Multiply this recipe by three and you've got yourself a three-layer cake.

PEAR & GINGER CARAMEL CAKE

TIMING

PREP 20 mins

BAKING approx.
30 mins

CHILLING 2 hours

MAKES 1 x 18 cm (7 in)
three-layer cake

SERVES approx. 18

INGREDIENTS

2 recipes Salted
Caramel (page 129)

3–4 whole pears

500 g (1 lb 2 oz)
plain flour

100 g (3½ oz)
cornflour

425 g (15 oz) brown
sugar

35 g (1¼ oz) baking
powder

285 g (10 oz) butter,
at room temperature

5 eggs

370 ml (13 fl oz) milk

50 ml (1½ fl oz)
canola oil

1½ teaspoons vanilla
extract

2 tablespoons
ground ginger

To decorate

2 recipes Vanilla
Bean Swiss Meringue
Buttercream
(page 107)

dehydrated pear
slices or slices of
glacé ginger

A shout-out to my staff for this beauty. This cake was baked by Sarah and iced by Sam; I am so proud to have them as part of the Magnolia Kitchen team. You all inspire me to be the boss I am, and I couldn't ask for more enthusiastic, caring and valuable staff to work alongside me at Magnolia Kitchen Sweet Cafe. Don't worry, Abby, I haven't forgotten you—without you taking my 'empty cup' hints and delivering repeat coffees, manning the coffee machine, greeting each customer with your kind-hearted and genuine welcoming smile, and serving up some bomb-ass caffeine it wouldn't matter how good the cakes/treats are. In fact, without the whole Magnolia Kitchen team, including my daughter Charlotte, this book—and the photo-shoot especially— wouldn't have been possible. My team are the best cake fluffers ever (if you don't know what a fluffer is, just have a wee google and think 'cake prep' not 'cock prep'). They literally baked whatever I requested, delivered the food for photographing, cleared it away afterwards and basically just were good bitches and kept Magnolia Kitchen running. xx

METHOD

Prepare your caramel ahead of time and set it aside.

Preheat your oven to 170°C (325°F). Prep three 18 cm (7 in) cake tins with cooking spray and line them with baking paper.

Cut your pears into quarters and remove the cores. Slice thinly, about 2 mm (¹⁄₁₆ in), and lay in a single layer in the bottom of each cake tin. Cover the pears with caramel—just enough to cover them slightly, don't go too crazy. You just want enough caramel to really caramelise the pears while the cake is baking. Set the rest of the caramel to one side.

Place the flour, cornflour, sugar and baking powder in the bowl of a stand mixer fitted with the paddle attachment, and mix on low to combine. Chop the butter into cubes, add it to the dry ingredients and keep mixing on low until the mixture resembles breadcrumbs. (If you must, do this by hand— but see my notes in the vanilla bean cake recipe, page 61.)

Continued overleaf

In a separate bowl, mix together the wet ingredients until combined (just the eggs, milk, oil and vanilla—not the remaining caramel; calm down and I'll tell you what to do with that soon . . . sheesh!). Add two-thirds of the wet mixture to the dry ingredients, and mix on medium-high until thick and fluffy. Add the remaining wet ingredients and mix well until combined and fluffy.

Scoop the mixture evenly over the pears and caramel in the tins (use your scales to get them all the same; see my tips on page 25), then drizzle 3-ish generous tablespoons of caramel over the batter in each tin. Using a cake poker (i.e. skewer or needle), gently swirl the caramel around in the batter. You don't want to mix it in, just swirl it through.

Bake for about 30 mins, until the cakes are golden brown and a skewer comes out clean when you poke it into the middle of each cake. Allow to cool in the tins for 5–10 mins, then turn out onto cooling racks.

When nice and cool, wrap the cakes in plastic wrap and chill for 2 hours (or overnight), as this will make them easier to trim and decorate.

Now, add your ground ginger to the remaining caramel and set aside—you'll use this when icing the cake. Prepare your Swiss meringue buttercream, and set it aside at room temp until your cake is completely chilled.

Ice your cake following my instructions on pages 68–75, using your ginger caramel as a filling between your layers. Decorate the top of the cake with dollops of buttercream around the edge—this will act as a dam for the generous amount of ginger caramel I am about to tell you to pour on top of the cake. Pour HEAPS of the caramel on top of the cake and spread out with a spatula. Decorate the icing dollops with slices of dehydrated pear or glacé ginger.

OPPOSITE The cake fluffers: Sam, Sarah and Abby. (What y'all laughing at?)

STRAWBERRY & PISTACHIO CAKE

TIMING

PREP 20 mins

BAKING approx. 30 mins

CHILLING 2 hours

MAKES 1 x 13 cm (5 in) three-layer cake

SERVES approx. 14

INGREDIENTS

150 g (5½ oz) raw shelled pistachios

300 g (10½ oz) plain flour

255 g (9 oz) caster sugar

24 g (⅞ oz) baking powder

170 g (6 oz) butter, at room temperature

3 eggs

240 ml (8 fl oz) milk

60 ml (2 fl oz) canola oil

1 teaspoon vanilla extract

200 g (7 oz) frozen (or fresh) strawberries

To decorate

see suggestions overleaf

METHOD

Preheat your oven to 180°C (350°F), prepare three 13 cm (5 in) cake tins with cooking spray and line them with baking paper.

Put your pistachios in a blender and blend until fine, making sure you don't overblend them and get nut butter. Put them through a sieve to remove any persistent chunky nuts—you can blend these again (and sieve again), or keep them for decorating (or just stick those nuts in yo' mouth).

Place all the dry ingredients, including the ground pistachios, in the bowl of a stand mixer fitted with the paddle attachment and mix on low to combine. Chop your butter into cubes, add it to the dry ingredients and mix on low until the mixture resembles breadcrumbs. I love this technique so much—it just feels like life is more simple this way (though you can also do this by hand, see the Vanilla Bean Cake recipe on page 61).

In a separate bowl, mix together the wet ingredients (not the strawberries, obviously) until combined. Add two-thirds of the wet mixture to the dry ingredients, and mix on medium-high until thick and fluffy. Add the remaining wet ingredients and mix well until combined, thick and fluffy. You can't beat this too much, so really beat the shit out of it to get that thick but fluffy consistency.

Scoop mixture evenly into the prepared tins (use your scales to get them all the same; see my tips on page 25). Finely chop your frozen strawberries and distribute evenly among the tins. Bake for about 30 mins, until the cakes are golden brown and a skewer poked into them comes out clean. Allow to cool in the tins for 5–10 mins, then turn out onto cooling racks.

Wrap your cooled cakes in plastic wrap and chill them for 2 hours (or overnight), to make them easier to trim and ice. Ice your cake with buttercream as shown in the instructional on pages 68–75.

OPPOSITE A dessert-sized serve of my Strawberry & Pistachio Cake (see pages 26–27 for my guide to serving sizes).

Continued overleaf

DECORATION

The sky is the limit in terms of decorating this cake. You may want to leave it simply finished with sharp-as-shit buttercream and top it with leftover chopped pistachios and freeze-dried strawberries, or you could get a li'l bit fancy up in the hiz-ouse like I have with this cute-as-F kitty cat design.

For the simple decoration, use 1 recipe Vanilla Bean Swiss Meringue Buttercream (page 104) or Strawberry Swiss Meringue Buttercream (page 107), with 1 recipe Strawberry Compote (page 135) as your filling, plus the leftover chopped pistachios and freeze-dried strawberries.

If you have chosen to be extra like me, here are some easy tips for the kitty cake. Ice your cake with Vanilla Bean Swiss Meringue Buttercream, and once you have your sharp-as-shit buttercream put the cake back in the fridge while you prep the decorations.

You will need modelling chocolate for the ears, fresh flowers, florists' tape, edible paint, a small food-safe paintbrush, a small amount of buttercream in a piping bag with a small piping tip (I used top #22), and a selection of sprinkles.

Knead your modelling chocolate until it is soft and resembles playdough consistency. Roll it out to about 5 mm (¼ in) thick, then cut into even triangles in proportion to the cake. Curve these so that they aren't completely flat.

Choose the flowers you want and trim the stems so that you have at least 5–7 cm (2–3 in) of stem. Wrap the ends of each stem in florists' tape to seal the cut end and protect the cake against contamination.

Take the cake out of the fridge and use the edible paint to paint a cute-as-F cat face on the front of the cake.

Pipe small dollops of buttercream where you want the ears to go, then place the moulded ears on top. Use edible paint to colour inside the ears if you wish. Pipe swirls of buttercream around the ears and add a few random dollops. Position your flowers around the ears, pushing the stems into the cake. I like to add more on one side than the other— personal aesthetics. Finally, add a few sprinkles around the ears and the top of the cake.

COCONUT TAMARILLO CAKE

TIMING

PREP 20 mins

BAKING approx. 30 mins

CHILLING 2 hours

MAKES 1 x 18 cm (7 in) three-layer cake

SERVES approx. 18

INGREDIENTS

6 tamarillos

500 g (1 lb 2 oz) plain flour

100 g (3½ oz) cornflour

425 g (15 oz) caster sugar

150 g (5½ oz) desiccated coconut

35 g (1¼ oz) baking powder

285 g (10 oz) butter, at room temperature

5 eggs

370 ml (13 fl oz) milk

50 ml (1½ fl oz) canola oil

1½ teaspoons vanilla extract

To decorate

1 recipe Tamarillo Curd (page 125)

1 recipe German Custard Buttercream (page 111)

tamarillo-coloured gel food colour*

deep red dried rose petals

METHOD

Prepare the Tamarillo Curd ahead of time, as you want this to be completely cool when you use it to layer your cake.

Preheat your oven to 170°C (325°F). Prep three 18 cm (7 in) cake tins with cooking spray and line them with baking paper. Peel your tamarillos and slice them thinly, about 2 mm (1⁄16 in), and lay in a single layer in the bottom of each cake tin.

Place all your dry ingredients in the bowl of a stand mixer fitted with the paddle attachment, and mix on low to combine. Chop the butter into cubes, add to the dry ingredients and mix on low until the mixture resembles breadcrumbs. (You *can* do this by hand—see the Vanilla Bean Cake recipe on page 61—but seriously, get a stand mixer!)

In a separate bowl, mix together the wet ingredients until combined. Add two-thirds of this wet mixture to the dry ingredients, and mix on medium-high until thick and fluffy. Add the remaining wet ingredients and *beat* well until combined and fluffy.

Scoop the mixture evenly over the tamarillos in the tins, using your scales to get the cakes the same size (see my tips on page 25). Bake for about 30 mins, until the cakes are golden brown and a skewer poked into them comes out clean. Allow to cool in the tins for 5–10 mins, then turn out onto cooling racks.

When the cakes are cool, wrap them in plastic wrap and chill for 2 hours (or overnight)—this will make them easier to trim and ice.

Prepare your German custard buttercream. When your cakes are chilled, ice them as per my instructions on pages 68–75, using your tamarillo curd for the filling. Decorate as per my instructions on pages 76–77, using the tamarillo-coloured gel food colour and dried rose petals.

* If you are unsure about what to use, my default tamarillo colour is burgundy.

CHRISTMAS CAKE

The fruit mince for this cake needs to be prepared weeks in advance, so bear this in mind when planning your baking!

TIMING

PREP 25 mins

BAKING 30–45 mins

CHILLING 2 hours

MAKES 1 x 18 cm (7 in) three-layer cake

SERVES approx. 18

INGREDIENTS

4 eggs

200 g (7 oz) butter, melted

440 g (15½ oz) plain flour

280 g (10 oz) soft brown sugar

2½ teaspoons baking soda

1 teaspoon ground cinnamon

2 teaspoons mixed spice

½ teaspoon ground nutmeg

1 recipe Christmas Fruit Mince (page 139)

180 g (6½ oz) brandy

To decorate

900 g (2 lb) White Chocolate Ganache, ratio 1:2 (page 115)

2 teaspoons almond essence (add this to taste)

shelled pistachios, dried cranberries, nuts and freeze-dried fruit of your choice

OPPOSITE If you are feeling a bit extra, you can add strawflowers and sprinkles of little gold cachous.

METHOD

Preheat your oven to 160°C (315°F). Prep three 18 cm (7 in) cake tins with cooking spray and line them with baking paper.

Put the eggs in your stand mixer and whisk until light and fluffy. Switch to the paddle attachment, add the melted butter and stir slowly to combine. Add the dry ingredients and beat slowly to combine. Now add the fruit mince and stir slowly to combine.

Divide the mixture evenly among the tins (use your scales to get them the same; see my tips on page 25), then bake for about 40 mins or until you can poke the cakes with a skewer and it comes out cleanish. It won't come out totally clean because of the fruit in the mix, but you shouldn't see any uncooked cake mix on the skewer.

Remove the cooked cakes from the oven and use your skewer to prick the cakes all over their tops. Pour 60 g (2¼ oz) of brandy evenly over each cake while still hot. Turn out onto plastic wrap and wrap tightly. Using the brandy and wrapping them while warm will keep them nice and moist. Allow to cool, then place in the fridge to chill for at least 2 hours to make them easier to trim and ice.

Meanwhile, make your ganache, then add the almond essence to taste and mix it through. Allow the ganache to set while the cakes chill. If your cakes are domed on top you will need to trim them (see page 68).

Soften your ganache by zapping it in the microwave in 10- to 20-second bursts, stirring in between, until it is a spreadable consistency. Smear a small amount of ganache onto a cake board that is 2.5 cm (1 in) larger in diameter than your cake. Place the first layer of cake onto the board and centre it. Dollop one-third of the icing on top and use an offset spatula to spread it around evenly until it reaches the edge of the cake. Place the next cake layer on top and repeat. When you have all three layers stacked, dollop the remaining icing on top and spread it evenly, bringing the icing right to the edge.

Decorate with the pistachios, cranberries, nuts and freeze-dried fruit, arranging them around the top edge of the cake.

ALLERGY-FRIENDLY MINI CAKES

TIMING

PREP 20 mins

BAKING approx. 20 mins

MAKES approx. 12

INGREDIENTS

240 g (8½ oz) coconut milk

80 g (2¾ oz) canola oil

1 tablespoon cider vinegar

1 teaspoon vanilla extract

1 teaspoon good-quality vanilla bean paste

220 g (7¾ oz) gluten-free flour

200 g (7 oz) caster sugar

1 teaspoon baking soda

1 pinch salt

Plum topping

200 g (7 oz) canned Black Doris plums, drained

To decorate

1 recipe Allergy-friendly Swiss Meringue Buttercream (page 108)

10 g (¼ oz) freeze-dried plums

METHOD

Prepare your allergy-friendly Swiss meringue buttercream and set it to one side.

Preheat your oven to 170°C (325°F). Prep a square mini cake tray with baking spray (I use a silicone one that is like a muffin tray but squares). You could use a round muffin tray if you want.

Place the wet ingredients (including both vanillas) in the bowl of your stand mixer and mix by hand to combine. Fit the whisk attachment, add the dry ingredients and mix to combine. Be aware that this batter is wetter than our other recipes—this is perfectly normal.

Using a medium-sized cookie scoop, divide the mixture evenly into the tray holes, filling each about two-thirds full. For the plum topping, place half a plum on top of each cake. Bake for about 20 mins, or until the mini cakes are golden and a skewer comes out cleanish when poked into them. Allow to cool in the tray.

Re-whip your buttercream so that it is soft and fluffy. Transfer it to a piping bag with a star tip, and pipe a swirl of icing on top of each cake. Decorate with crushed pieces of freeze-dried plum.

VARIATIONS

- You can make this recipe into a full-sized cake—multiply the recipe by three, place in three 18 cm (7 in) lined round cake tins and bake for about 30 mins.
- Add spices, fruit and/or nuts to create a multitude of deliciousness.

ICINGS,
CURDS &
FILLINGS

—

SWISS MERINGUE BUTTERCREAM

TIMING
PREP/MIXING 20–30 mins

MAKES approx. 950 g (2 lb 2 oz)

INGREDIENTS
200 g (7 oz) egg whites

250 g (9 oz) caster sugar

425 g (15 oz) butter, at room temperature

METHOD
Place the egg whites and sugar in a heatproof bowl—I do this in my metal stand-mixer bowl, 'cause I'm a 'make minimal washing up' kinda gal. (If you have a double boiler use that, but seriously, I've never even seen one of those elusive contraptions.)

Grab a pot that is smaller than your bowl. Fill the pot half full of water and bring it to the boil, then turn it down to a simmer. Rest your bowl on top of the pot, and put a large spoon in the pot so that the steam can escape between the bowl and pot. Keeping the water just simmering, stir the stuff in the bowl until the sugar has dissolved into the egg white. To test this, dunk your thumb and pointer finger in and rub them together—this is gross, as it feels like snot, but it's the best way to test. You don't want to be feeling any gritty bits of sugar.

Once your sugar has dissolved, transfer the gloop to your mixer bowl if you haven't already. Fit the whisk attachment and mix on high until you get stiff peaks. You can also use a hand-held electric beater, but I wouldn't recommend beating this by hand as you'll end up with a very tired arm and a sloppy meringue.

While your meringue is beating, prepare your room-temp butter by cutting it into cubes of about 2.5 cm (1 in).

When you have your stiff peaks, start adding the butter one cube at a time to the meringue while continuing to mix on high. Now, LISTEN UP AS THIS IS IMPORTANT! You'll notice that after the first few cubes of butter have been added, your meringue will flop and become sloppy. DO NOT PANIC! Just keep adding the butter, one cube at a time (trust me, I'm a professional). When all the butter has been added, keep mixing on high, and before your very eyes your sloppy, curdled cottage-cheese-looking mess will transform into a beautiful, silky-smooth Swiss meringue buttercream.

Now that you're all like 'Bets, you're fucken amazing, I'm glad I listened', it's time to flavour. Add your desired flavour as per the inspo on page 107, and mix to combine. TA DA!

GERMAN CUSTARD BUTTERCREAM

TIMING

PREP/MIXING 20–30 mins

MAKES approx. 1.7 kg (3 lb 12 oz)

INGREDIENTS

900 g (2 lb) butter, at room temperature

1 recipe Vanilla Bean Custard (page 136)

This is a great buttercream for those who don't like a super-sweet icing, and is an acclaimed favourite of Mr Gee's. It's great paired with our peach cake (page 62), layered up with a fresh custard filling inside the buttercream. If you're feeling fancy as fuck, add some crushed shortbread between the layers too!

METHOD

Chop your butter into cubes of about 2.5 cm (1 in) and set to one side.

Make the Vanilla Bean Custard, and while it's still warm put it into the bowl of your stand mixer. Using the whisk attachment, whisk the custard on high to cool it. When your mixer bowl is warm to the touch (not hot), start adding your butter a few cubes at a time. Allow each addition to incorporate before adding more.

Once all the butter is added and combined, change to the paddle attachment and beat on medium for a further 5 mins to allow the buttercream to become fluffy.

This can be flavoured along the same lines as any of our other buttercreams—see page 107.

CREAM CHEESE ICING

TIMING

PREP/MIXING 20–30 mins

MAKES approx. 500 g (1 lb 2 oz)

INGREDIENTS

250 g (9 oz) butter, at room temperature

250 g (9 oz) traditional cream cheese

100-150 g (3½–5½ oz) icing sugar, sifted

METHOD

Beat your butter (ideally in a stand mixer with a scraper attachment) until it is fluffy and whitened. Cut the cream cheese into 2.5 cm (1 in) cubes and add these, one at a time, to the butter while the mixer is going. Let each cube incorporate fully before adding more.

Stop the mixer, scrape down the sides and start adding your sifted icing sugar. Start with 100 g (3½ oz) and beat this in until combined. Have a sneaky taste test—if this is how you like your cream cheese icing, then don't add any more icing sugar. If you prefer a sweeter cream cheese icing, then add the extra and beat it in well. You don't want more than the amount I listed, or your cream cheese icing will get nasty: sort of grainy and crusty. I am such a purist when it comes to cream cheese icing—nothing infuriates me more than cake that says it's iced with cream cheese but in reality it tastes like licking a beach where the salt has been replaced with sugar. YUK!

Add your flavouring (see below) and beat for a further 5 mins on high to combine.

LEMON CREAM CHEESE ICING
2 tablespoons lemon juice
2 teaspoons lemon zest

VANILLA BEAN CREAM CHEESE ICING
1 teaspoon vanilla extract
¼ teaspoon good-quality vanilla bean paste

CHOCOLATE GANACHE

TIMING

PREP/MIXING 30 mins

SETTING varies (see notes overleaf)

MAKES approx. 300 g (10½ oz)

**INGREDIENTS
(1:2 RATIO)**

100 g (3½ oz) cream

200 g (7 oz) chopped chocolate (dark or white)

Ganache can be made in different ratios of chocolate to cream, and is allowed to set for different times depending on what you're using it for. Read the notes below and overleaf before you start, as this will affect your timings!

METHOD

Heat the cream in a pot on your stove until it starts to bubble around the edges of the pot—try not to let it boil, as it will burn in seconds.

While the cream is heating, put your chocolate in a heatproof (and preferably microwave-safe) bowl. When the cream is ready, remove it from the heat and pour it directly over the chocolate.

Allow it to rest for approx. 5 mins—this will allow the cream to melt the chocolate. Then use a spatula to stir it together until your ganache resembles a smooth, silky, luscious, chocolatey delight that you could just dive into.

Keep the ganache in a bowl or an airtight container at room temperature until you're ready to use it. Always cover it with plastic wrap pushed flat onto the top of the ganache, as this will stop a crusty, crystallised skin forming that can make the ganache taste gritty.

ALL ABOUT RATIOS

There are different ratios of cream to chocolate for different uses. The 1:2 ratio in the recipe above means 1 part cream to 2 parts chocolate.

DARK CHOCOLATE GANACHE RATIOS
- 1:1 for a glaze
- 1:2 for cake filling and piping
- 1:3 for covering cake (if stored at room temp)
- 1:4 for covering cake (if stored at room temp in the heat of summer)

WHITE CHOCOLATE GANACHE RATIOS
- 1:1 for a glaze
- 1:2 for cake filling and piping
- 1:4 for covering cake (if stored at room temp)
- 1:5 for covering cake (if stored at room temp in the heat of summer)

Obviously, different ratios make different amounts of ganache. Here's a table with some useful quantities. Choose the ratio you want, then look down that column for the amount that's nearest to what you need. You may have to do some maths on occasion!

1:1 RATIO

200 g ganache
= 100 g cream + 100 g chocolate

300 g ganache
= 150 g cream + 150 g chocolate

400 g ganache
= 200 g cream + 200 g chocolate

600 g ganache
= 300 g cream + 300 g chocolate

1:3 RATIO

400 g ganache
= 100 g cream + 300 g chocolate

600 g ganache
= 150 g cream + 450 g chocolate

800 g ganache
= 200 g cream + 600 g chocolate

1.2 kg ganache
= 300 g cream + 900 g chocolate

1:2 RATIO

300 g ganache
= 100 g cream + 200 g chocolate

450 g ganache
= 150 g cream + 300 g chocolate

600 g ganache
= 200 g cream + 400 g chocolate

900 g ganache
= 300 g cream + 600 g chocolate

1:4 RATIO

500 g ganache
= 100 g cream + 400 g chocolate

750 g ganache
= 150 g cream + 600 g chocolate

1 kg ganache
= 200 g cream + 800 g chocolate

1.5 kg ganache
= 300 g cream + 1.2 kg chocolate

SETTING TIMES FOR VARIOUS USES

- For a glaze, use straight away.
- For filling and piping, allow to set at room temperature until the ganache is spreadable like room-temp butter.
- For covering cakes, allow to set until solid. To use, cut into 2.5 cm (1 in) squares, put these in a suitable bowl and heat in the microwave in bursts of 10–20 seconds, stirring in between bursts, until your ganache is a spreadable consistency. This method will allow you to prep the ganache ahead of time and use it as required.

ALLERGY-FRIENDLY VARIATION

For an allergy-friendly variation on Dark Chocolate Ganache, replace the cream with either hot water or coconut cream, and ensure that your dark chocolate is dairy-free. Usually 50% cocoa and higher is dairy-free, but always check the label. Make the ganache the same way as on the previous page. Have a look at the dark chocolate flavour inspos opposite, too.

FLAVOUR INSPO FOR CHOCOLATE GANACHE

HAZELNUT DARK CHOCOLATE GANACHE
Add 1–2 teaspoons hazelnut oil to your ganache when it is a soft consistency, and mix to combine.

ORANGE DARK CHOCOLATE GANACHE
Add ¼ teaspoon orange oil to your ganache when it is a soft consistency, and mix to combine.

PEPPERMINT DARK CHOCOLATE GANACHE
Add ¼ teaspoon peppermint oil to your ganache when it is a soft consistency, and mix to combine.

ESPRESSO CHOCOLATE GANACHE
Add a double shot of espresso to your ganache when it is a soft consistency, and mix to combine. Alternatively, dissolve 1–2 teaspoons instant coffee in your cream before heating it.

FRUIT WHITE CHOCOLATE GANACHE
Add fruit compote or jams to your ganache when it is a soft consistency, and mix well to combine. The quantity you add will vary depending on your personal taste, so start with less and add more if required.

LEMON WHITE CHOCOLATE GANACHE
Add ½ teaspoon lemon oil and the zest of 1 lemon to your ganache when it is a soft consistency, and mix to combine.

VANILLA BEAN WHITE CHOCOLATE GANACHE
Add ¼ teaspoon good-quality vanilla bean paste and 1 teaspoon vanilla extract to your ganache when it is a soft consistency, and mix to combine.

CHOCOLATE MIRROR GLAZE

TIMING

PREP 20 mins

MAKES enough to glaze a round 18 cm (7 in) 3-layer cake

INGREDIENTS

10 g (¼ oz) powdered gelatine

60 g (2¼ oz) cold water

150 g (5½ oz) caster sugar

150 g (5½ oz) glucose

75 g (2½ oz) water

100 g (3½ oz) sweetened condensed milk

150 g (5½ oz) chopped white or dark chocolate

This is the glaze I've used for the chocolate cake pictured on page 64. Y'all ready for this? It's magical.

METHOD

Mix the gelatine and 60 g (2¼ oz) water together, and set aside to bloom.

Put the sugar, glucose, second quantity of water and condensed milk in a pot, and heat on low, stirring frequently. Keep heating and stirring until the sugar is dissolved, then remove from the heat and add the bloomed gelatine, stirring it in until completely melted.

Add the chocolate and combine until melted, using a stick blender to remove any bubbles—keep the stick blender in one place, allowing the glaze to be sucked into it evenly. At this point you can colour the glaze with any food colour gel. If I'm making it with white chocolate, I like to whiten it first using a titanium-based food colour gel to give it an opaque look before colouring.

MIRROR GLAZING STEP BY STEP

———

Ice your cake with buttercream as per the instructions on pages 68–75; any of our buttercreams will work for this recipe. When you reach the end of the icing instructions, place your cake in the freezer for about 1 hour. The trick is to have your cake super-chill so that the temp of the glaze does not melt the buttercream as it drizzles my nizzle down the hizzle. Know what I'm-a saying fo shizzle. OK, carry on with the following steps for mirror glazing and remember that you CAN'T CONTROL THIS DESIGN. The beauty is in the randomness.

I have chosen white as the base colour for this step-by-step, with feature colours of peach and grey. Prep these before you start: pour 40 g (1½ oz) of Mirror Glaze into a couple of separate vessels. Add your desired food colour (you can use powders or gels)—remember that these colours will mix with the main colour, so make sure they are strong.

Continued overleaf

1. Set up a shallow baking tray and ensure that your mirror glazes are ready to go. Place a small bowl upside down in the baking tray, this shit's gon' get messy. Remove your cake from the freezer. Don't leave it sitting out too long, as condensation will collect on the cake and the glaze will slip off in places. Place your cake on top of the bowl. Pour your main block colour glaze (mine's white here) over the top of the cake. The glaze will pool at the top and drizzle down the sides. Keep pouring until the cake is covered with glaze down to the bottom.

2. Pour on a small amount of your second colour (peach) in a circular drizzle.

3. Pour on your third colour (grey) over the top in a circular drizzle. The glaze will start swirling and moving down the cake in a glorious marble design.

4. Repeat steps 2 and 3, adding more of each colour. Ensure that there is enough glaze on the cake to cover all the buttercream.

5. Using a cake detailing palette knife, swipe gently across the top of the glaze.

6. OOOH—AHHHHH! The beauty of the glaze, so random and so beautiful. The glaze needs to set, so move the baking tray along with the cake (still on the bowl) CAREFULLY into the fridge. Allow to set for about 2 hours. The glaze will remain sticky but will resemble jelly. When you're ready to serve, grab a thicker cake board, 5 mm (¼ in) thick and 2.5 cm (1 in) larger than your cake (so if your cake is 18 cm/7 in, the larger cake board will be 20 cm/8 in). Attach some double-sided tape to the larger board and transfer the glazed cake to the larger board, making sure that it is centred. You can stop here with the design, or you can add chocolate sculptures or fresh florals.

BASIC CITRUS CURD

TIMING

PREP 5-8 mins

COOKING 30-40 mins

MAKES approx. 500 g (1 lb 2 oz)

INGREDIENTS

160 g (5¾ oz) citrus juice (see options in headnote)

1 tablespoon citrus zest

85 g (3 oz) butter

2 egg yolks

2 whole eggs

220 g (7¾ oz) caster sugar

You can make this recipe with any citrus fruit—try lemons, oranges, blood oranges, tangarines, grapefruit, limes, etc. Use the curd to fill doughnuts or cakes, or add it to some warm brioche toast.

METHOD

Place all the ingredients in a blender (I find a smoothie blender is best), and blend on high until combined.

Pour into a pot and heat on low, stirring occasionally. Your curd will begin to produce large, slow-popping bubbles. By this stage it will have thickened. Remove it from the heat, transfer it to a clean jar, allow to cool and store in the fridge.

Yes, you read that right—no double boiler, no tempering eggs, no fucking around—literally just whack everything in the blender. I realise I've just turned every curd recipe on its head, and I'm not sorry in the slightest. I know that your brain is broken because EVERY staff member I hire is completely and utterly baffled that this method works. It goes against every ounce of their being and every second of their training. I love watching them try to get their educated, highly trained brains around how this could possibly succeed.

This recipe is dedicated to my girl Sam—may you always trust in 'the Bets', may your brain always be broken when I bring you a recipe I have quickly scribbled out and you test it and succeed, and may you always have me sitting on your shoulder no matter what kitchen you find yourself in, just telling you to FUCKEN WING IT. Books and learning are cool, okay, but creativity is key—so take your classical training and always add a dose of Bets. xx

BASIC FRUIT CURD

TIMING

PREP 5–8 mins

COOKING 30–40 mins

MAKES approx. 500 g
(1 lb 2 oz)

INGREDIENTS

2 whole eggs

2 egg yolks

85 g (3 oz) butter

75 g (2½ oz) caster
sugar

280 g (10 oz) fresh
or frozen fruit (see
suggestions below)

2 tablespoons lemon
juice

1 teaspoon lemon
zest

All my employees to date have had some sort of culinary and/or pastry chef training, so they have learnt something one way and been told that UNDER NO CIRCUMSTANCES should it be done another way or they will fail miserably. Then they walk into Magnolia Kitchen and see me cutting corners and quite literally making up shit like this curd recipe as I go along, with absolutely zero training really . . . it has them shaking their heads and (eventually) rolling their eyes. But just try it—TRUST ME, IT WORKS!

METHOD

Put all the ingredients in a blender (a smoothie blender is best for this amount) and blend on high until combined.

Pour into a pot and heat on low, stirring occasionally. By the time your curd begins to produce large, slow-popping bubbles, it will have thickened. Remove it from the heat, put it in a clean jar, let it cool and store it in the fridge.

If you are making the curd with pink or red fruits, add 1 or 2 drops of red food colour while cooking, to give the curd a more vibrant colour—pink/red fruits tend to go brown when curded.

FRUIT SUGGESTIONS

- Tamarillo Curd (pictured opposite): scoop the tamarillo flesh out of the skins until you have the right quantity.
- Strawberry Curd
- Raspberry Curd
- Rhubarb and Strawberry Curd: use half rhubarb and half strawberry, e.g. 140 g (5 oz) of each. Spread rhubarb stalks over a baking tray, cover with a sprinkling of sugar and roast at 160°C (315°F) until soft and mushy. Allow to cool, then weigh out the right amount.
- Peach Curd: canned peaches work well for this—rinse before using.
- Mango Curd
- Black Doris Plum Curd: canned plums work well; remove the stones before cooking.
- Apple Curd: peel and core your apples, dice into small pieces (1 cm/½ in) and cook with 2 tablespoons of water until the apple is soft and mushy. Allow to cool before making your curd.

PASSIONFRUIT CURD

TIMING

PREP 5–8 mins

COOKING 30–40 mins

MAKES approx. 400 g (14 oz)

INGREDIENTS

125 g (4½ oz) passionfruit pulp

3 eggs

80 g (2¾ oz) butter

100 g (3½ oz) caster sugar

1 tablespoon lemon juice

This is another easy-as-shit curd recipe. It probably looks wrong to you, but it WORKS. Trust me. You can use this curd to fill cakes or doughnuts or to flavour buttercream.

METHOD

Strain the seeds from the passionfruit pulp and set them aside. Put the pulp and all the other ingredients in a blender (preferably a smoothie blender) and blend on high until combined.

Pour into a pot and heat on low, stirring occasionally. Your curd will begin to produce large, slow-popping bubbles, by which time it will have thickened.

Remove it from the heat and stir in the reserved seeds. Transfer to a clean jar, allow to cool and store in the fridge.

FRUIT COMPOTE

TIMING

COOKING approx. 30 mins

MAKES approx. 300 g (10½ oz)

INGREDIENTS

280 g (10 oz) frozen fruit (see flavour suggestions)

100 g (3½ oz) caster sugar

squeeze of citrus juice

We use this to fill doughnuts, between layers of cake, as toppings for mini cakes, and for adding to buttercream and ganache.

METHOD

Put all the ingredients in a pot and heat on low until the fruit has become mush and has reduced by half. If it needs help becoming mush, use a potato masher to give the fruit a quick mash to make it mushier. Cool, then store in a jar in the fridge.

FLAVOUR SUGGESTIONS

- Mango and passionfruit (equal quantities)
- Strawberry
- Boysenberry
- Blackberry
- Raspberry (pictured)
- Mango
- Peach
- Rhubarb and strawberry (equal quantities)

VANILLA BEAN CUSTARD

TIMING

PREP/COOKING
25 mins

MAKES approx. 800 g
(1 lb 12 oz)

INGREDIENTS

450 g (1 lb) milk

½ teaspoon good-quality vanilla bean paste

280 g (10 oz) caster sugar

42 g (1½ oz) cornflour

2 whole eggs

2 egg yolks

This custard was designed for making my German Custard Buttercream (page 111). Along the way it earnt my respect as a stand-alone recipe. It can be used to fill doughnuts, used as a filling between layers of cake or served warm with fresh berries as an easy dessert.

METHOD

Put the milk and vanilla in a pot and bring to a simmer over a low heat.

In a separate bowl, whisk together the sugar, cornflour, whole eggs and yolks until nicely combined. When the milk is hot but not boiling, pour a quarter of it into the egg mixture and stir in—this tempers the eggs.

Return the milk pot to the heat and, while whisking, start slowly adding the egg mixture to the pot. Continue whisking constantly until the mixture is combined. It will gradually start to thicken.

When it thickens to a thick yoghurt consistency, like you could spoon it directly into your mouth without it dripping everywhere (BUT DON'T DO THIS, IT'S FUCKEN HOT—this description is for consistency purposes), remove it from the heat and give it one last *whisk whisk whisk* to make sure it's nice and smooth. Transfer to a container or bowl, and press plastic wrap against the custard to stop a skin forming. Allow to cool completely before using, unless you want it for German Custard Buttercream (page 111), in which case you can go straight to that recipe while the custard is hot.

- My favourite nozzle for macarons is a round Wilton 2A metal nozzle, and I now use biodegradable piping bags.
- I am on team baking paper all the way. Silicone mats are hopeless and don't get me started on those silly silicone mould mats—DON'T FALL FOR THOSE. With oven trays, I've always had success with aluminium.

INGREDIENTS

- Every batch of almond meal is different! This is bloody annoying because it means there is an element of winging it that really is unavoidable. The best thing to do is get *really* familiar with WHAT THE MACARONAGE LOOKS AND FEELS LIKE! (The macaronage is the paste you get when you mix together the dry ingredients and the egg white, and I am yelling this because in my experience this is the most valuable tip I have taught myself and my staff.)

  Me: Why are these macarons fucked?
  Staff: New batch of almond meal.
  Me: Son of a bitch WHHHYYYYYYYYYYYYYY?

- Adding things to the macaronage for flavour can change the outcome drastically. I have found that there is a perfect quantity of cocoa: too much and they're fucked (often soggy and wrinkly), too little and they're basically vanilla. Freeze-dried fruit powders can make the feet (the delicate, frilly layer at the base of a macaron shell) really frothy—instead of going up they go out, and your macarons look like they're wearing a tutu. I love LorAnn products for flavouring macarons, as you don't need much to get a good flavour profile and it doesn't compromise the consistency.

COLOURS

- Personally I prefer pastel colours that just hint at the flavour, but only because I *hate* eating food that has so much food colour in it that it colours your whole mouth. If you are going for a pastel colour, I recommend gel colours added to the macaronage. Always go darker than what you want to end up with, because the meringue will whiten it right down and by the time you realise this it will be too late. DO NOT COLOUR AFTER THE MERINGUE IS ADDED.
- If a really deep colour *is* required, I like to use coloured powders. Weirdly, I also find airbrush food colouring very good. It is super-liquid and concentrated.
- For really vibrant colours or black, add the colour to the sugar syrup. If you're using liquid colour, make sure you reduce the water quantity by the amount of food colour you're adding. I colour the macaronage too, for extra security.

TECHNIQUE

- In lots of recipes, the description for your perfect macaron mixture will be 'ribbon effect' or 'resembling lava'. I used to yell at every instruction for macarons that used those terms, I was always so infuriated. I'd be screaming 'what the fuck even IS a fucken ribbon of macaron mixture . . . seriously, WHAT?' Y'all know I use those terms in here, right, because now I am *awesome* I totally get it. Your perfect mixture will fall off your spatula just like a ribbon and it will be a beautiful thing. Lucky I made Lottie, the photographer, take hundreds of photos just to capture the ribbon in action. See picture 9 in my Italian Macaron instructional (page 150) and say 'Thank you.'
- Oven temperature is important. You want there to be enough heat to slowly cook your macarons, but not so much that it browns them and not so little that they just never get up on their feet. Oven quirks that can immediately affect your macarons are oven lights, fan-bake setting and oven placement. Back when I perfected macarons in my home oven, I didn't use the oven lights and never used fan-bake, as these two things would cause my mac shells to be lopsided. And I could only cook one tray at a time, on the second level from the bottom. Needless to say, when I opened Magnolia Kitchen Sweet Cafe and levelled up to a commercial oven I thought I was going to have to start from scratch (not a happy thought) BUT the basic temperatures and timings were exactly the same. The only difference was that it was a fan oven, but for some reason that didn't make any difference (maybe there are commercial oven gods?).

DECORATION

- Sprinkling flavours and toppings on top of macarons before baking them can add an extra little somethin' somethin'. Be aware that freeze-dried fruits will often brown fast—your beautiful raspberries will become crusty brown things on your pretty macs. Chocolate will melt (duh), Nerds (lollies) will cause huge craters, and salt is great for a day or so but will attract moisture and eat away at the macaron, leaving a hole in the shell. Nuts work well, as do edible confetti, chia seeds, sprinkles or a dusting of cocoa.

OK, I think that's it . . . Go forth and macaron!

ITALIAN MACARON INSTRUCTIONAL

TIMING

PREP 20 mins

BAKING 12–15 mins

ICING & DECORATING 15–20 mins (with buttercream ready prepped)

MAKES approx. 44 shells = 22 macarons

INGREDIENTS

Basic macaronage

225 g (8 oz) almond meal

225 g (8 oz) icing sugar

225 g (8 oz) caster sugar

60 g (2¼ oz) water

2 x 83 g (3 oz) egg white

Goody Gum Drop macaron shells

½–1 teaspoon teal gel food colour

1 teaspoon cotton candy flavour (LorAnn)

Filling & decoration

1 recipe Vanilla Bean Swiss Meringue Buttercream (page 107)

200 g (7 oz) chopped white chocolate

50 g (1¾ oz) Jelly Tots

sprinkles (hundreds and thousands)

This recipe is my basic Holy Grail macaron recipe. It can be used for other flavours—actually I encourage that. For this instructional version I've transformed the basic recipe into my fun-loving goody gum drop macarons.

METHOD

First, have you read *Macarons According to Me* on pages 142–145? If not, do that now, because it's important.

Now you can start. Preheat your oven to between 125°C and 135°C (260–275°F).

1. Have all your equipment and ingredients ready. Line your baking tray with pre-cut non-stick baking paper laid over a macaron template. Put your almond meal and icing sugar in a blender and blend on high until combined—don't over-blend, as you will just heat the almonds and it will try to make almond butter, which (duh) won't work. You want your almonds and icing sugar to be combined, and the almonds to be blended finer than how you bought them. Set this aside.

2. Combine the caster sugar and water in a pot, and heat on medium high with your thermometer inserted. While this is heating, quickly put the first 83 g (3 oz) of egg white in your mixer bowl and fit the whisk attachment. Once your sugar syrup reaches about 115°C (240°F), turn your mixer on high to semi-whip your egg white.

3. Once your sugar syrup reaches 122°C (252°F), take it off the heat and, with the mixer still going, *slowly* pour the syrup down the side of the bowl into the semi-whipped egg white. DO NOT DUMP the syrup straight into the mixer—this shit is molten hot, and if you pour it over the whisk while it's spinning round and round you're going to make a hell of a mess as the syrup will just flick up the side of the bowl and never make it to the egg. Keep beating the meringue until the bowl is cool to the touch and the peaks hold stiff like a really stiff thing—you don't want a soft flop on your meringue. This can take 5–10 mins, so while the stiffening is in progress move to the next step. (Just keep a bit of an eye on the meringue while you do that.)

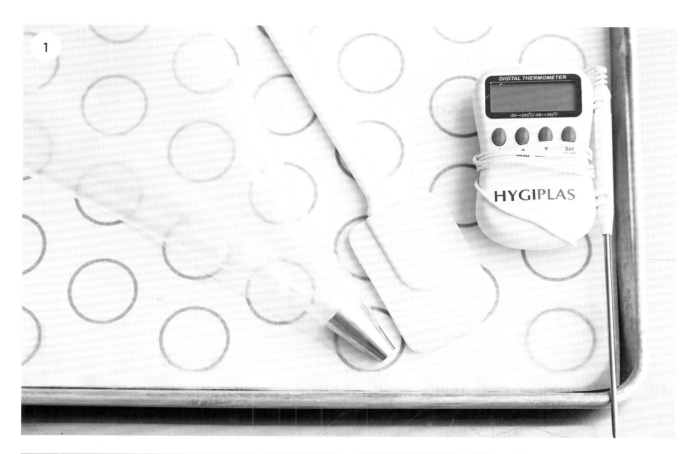

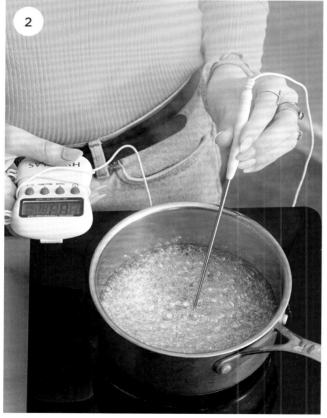

4. Put your blended almond and icing sugar in a wide bowl; I like to go large and use a bowl with a nice flat bottom. Add the remaining 83 g (3 oz) of egg white, plus any colour and flavours. For this instructional I added about 1 teaspoon of teal gel food colour (because I was heavy-handed), along with the LorAnn flavour. (Fun fact: cotton candy tastes exactly like Goody Goody Gum Drops ice cream—SECRET REVEALED.)

5. Mix until it resembles a thick paste. This is the macaronage, and this is where I am going to try to explain the most important visual cue. The macaronage needs to be a thick paste—mixing this will give you a work-out and this is where I find the wide, flat-bottomed bowl comes in handy. Use a *smearing* motion to get a macaronage that is uniform in consistency. You should be able to pick up a handful, roll it into a ball and have it hold its shape, but you should also be able to squish that ball without any cracks appearing. You don't want the mixture so thick that it's crumbly and dry. Start with the quantities I listed, and if needed then adjust based on my description above. If the mixture is too wet, add more almond meal in 15 g (½ oz) quantities, mixing each time until it reaches my described consistency. If it is crumbly and dry, add more egg white, 1 teaspoon at a time. Be careful not to add too much almond, or you'll have to counteract with more egg white so you'll be changing the recipe too much and I'm walking away.

6. Once your meringue is stiff as fuck—see the photo of me posing with my stiff meringue—stop the mixer. Add half the meringue to your bowl of macaronage.

7. With your spatula, use the same smearing motion to combine the macaronage and meringue until it is a uniform consistency. Think: *smear, scrape, fold . . . smear, scrape, fold.*

8. Add the remaining meringue, and now just scrape around the outside of the bowl and fold it in. Do this slowly and gently, so as not to overmix and destroy the meringue.

9. When your mixture is uniform in colour and texture and you can no longer see any meringue, fold a couple more times. It will be ready when you can drag your spatula through the bowl and the mixture will start to slowly move in on itself, like . . . hmmmmm, what is a great descriptive word that will explain this movement? Well, like LAVA—it will move in on itself like lava. Now scoop some mixture up onto your spatula and slowly let it fall from the spatula into the bowl—your mixture is perfection when it falls in a consistent slow 'ribbon' off the spatula. If you don't achieve ribbon status with your mixture, continue folding until this occurs.

10. Grab your piping bag. Trim the end and insert the piping nozzle, then twist the bag just above the nozzle to seal it at the bottom. Find an old vase or something similar you can put your piping bag in, and fold the open end over the edge to hold the bag open. Scrape your macaron mixture into your piping bag and twist the top of the bag closed to secure it.

11. Now you need your prepared baking tray. Use something like a piece of cutlery to weigh your paper down so it doesn't slide all over the place. Holding your piping bag at the twisted top, position it straight up and down with the nozzle approximately 1 centimetre (½ inch) off the paper in the centre of one of the guide circles. Use one hand to steady the nozzle and the other hand to squeeze the bag from the top. Squeeze gently until the mixture reaches just inside the outer edge of the guide, then stop squeezing and, with your nozzle still close to the macaron mixture, flick the nozzle in a small half-circle motion and pull up and away. Move to your next guide circle and repeat. This process will take practice, but you will soon find a piping technique that works for *you*.

12. *Carefully* remove the guide template from under your baking paper.

13. Lift the tray with one hand on each side, raise it off the bench about 8–10 centimetres (3–4 inches) and bang it down onto the bench. This will bring any air bubbles to the surface; repeat the banging until the bubbles have all risen and popped. I usually do this about five times, turning the tray so that each side gets a focused bang. Be careful not to bang at an angle or too vigorously—you can flick the paper over and all the mixture will stick together, and that is a real knicker-ripping result.

14. Put your macarons in your oven preheated to about 125°C (260°F)—YES, STRAIGHT IN THE OVEN. I set my timer for 14 mins (you may want to start at 12 mins). Just bake one tray at a time and place it in the middle of your oven; while the first tray is baking you can pipe the next tray.

When the timer goes off, you need to check if they are ready. Touch the top and give them a little wiggle—if they don't move they are ready, and if they move then put them back in for another minute. If you take them out when there is still movement in the feet, then the feet won't be cooked enough to support the weight of the shell and it will collapse when it's cooled. Repeat this until you are satisfied that those feet are stable. Remove the shells from the oven and allow them to cool on the paper. You can leave the macarons on the baking tray or you can slide them off (still on the paper) if you need to use the tray for more macarons.

15. Marry your shells with their perfect life partner that is exactly the same—remove all the shells from the paper, then grab two shells and hold them flat bum to flat bum. If they are the same then put them aside together, and continue until you have all your shells married up. Line them up in rows with one bum up, one top up.

If you are just here for the basic method, then go forth and fill to your heart's desire. If you're making Goody Gum Drop Macarons, let's continue. Put your ready-made buttercream in a clean piping bag with a large French star tip such as Ateco 867 or Wilton 88 (this is my signature Magnolia Kitchen macaron-filling nozzle). Pipe a dollop of buttercream onto each bum shell, using enough so that it nearly reaches the edge of the shell.

MOCHA ESPRESSO MACARONS

TIMING

PREP 20 mins

BAKING 12–15 mins

ICING & DECORATING
10–20 mins

MAKES approx. 44
shells = 22 macarons

INGREDIENTS
Macaron shells

225 g (8 oz) almond
meal

225 g (8 oz) icing
sugar

1 tablespoon (8 g)
Dutch cocoa

30 g (1 oz) espresso
coffee or 1 tablespoon
instant coffee

30 or 60 g (1 or
2¼ oz) water (see
method)

225 g (8 oz) caster
sugar

2 x 83 g (3 oz) egg
white

Filling

30 g (1 oz) espresso,
or 1 tablespoon instant
coffee dissolved in
1 tablespoon hot water

1 recipe Swiss
Meringue
Buttercream
(page 104)

50 g (1¾ oz) Dark
Chocolate Ganache
(page 115), ratio 1:2

OPPOSITE Mocha Espresso
and Strawberry Macarons.

METHOD

Important note: If you're an experienced macaron maker, just follow the steps below—you'll know how things should look. If you're new to this, however, then follow my step-by-step instructional (complete with awesome photos) on pages 146–153. Also, do read *Macarons According to Me* (pages 142–145) before you start.

Preheat your oven to between 125°C and 135°C (260–275°F). Get all your equipment and ingredients ready, and line your baking tray with pre-cut non-stick baking paper laid over a macaron template.

Blend your almond meal, icing sugar and cocoa on high until combined and the almond meal is a bit finer. The cocoa is there to balance the coffee you'll add to your sugar syrup.

Now for the sugar syrup. If using espresso, replace 30 g (1 oz) of the water with the 30 g (1 oz) of espresso. If using instant coffee, just add this straight to the 60 g (2¼ oz) water. Add the caster sugar, and mix to dissolve everything before heating. Now start heating the coffee/sugar mix, and put the first 83 g (3 oz) of egg white in your mixer bowl fitted with the whisk attachment. When the coffee syrup reaches about 115°C (240°F), start your egg white whipping. Once your coffee syrup reaches 122°C (252°F), slowly pour it down the side of the mixer bowl into the semi-whipped egg white, keeping the mixer going the whole time. Keep it beating until the bowl is cool and the meringue is good and stiff.

Meanwhile, start mixing the second 83 g (3 oz) of egg white into your blended almond mixture until it resembles a thick paste that you can roll into a ball and squish without cracks appearing. (Adjust as necessary with extra almond meal or egg white—but not too much.)

Add half the coffee-flavoured meringue to your macaronage, mixing with a smearing motion to get a nice uniform consistency. Add the remaining meringue, and slowly and gently fold it in until you have a mixture with a perfect 'ribbon' consistency. Transfer to your piping bag with its nozzle, twist the end closed and start piping. When done, carefully remove the template and bang the tray on the benchtop several times to remove the air bubbles.

Continued overleaf

Now put the tray of macarons straight into the middle of your preheated oven and set your timer (I set mine for 14 mins; you may want to start at 12). Check that the feet are cooked properly; if not, cook for a minute longer and check again. When they're done, let them cool on the paper, then marry up perfectly matching pairs of shells. Lay them out in rows with one bum up, one top up.

For the filling, add the espresso or dissolved instant coffee to your Swiss meringue buttercream. Mix either by hand or using your mixer until well combined.

Prepare your chocolate ganache as described on page 115.

Using your large French star tip for our signature macaron filling, pipe dollops of coffee buttercream onto your macaron bums. Add a dollop of dark chocolate ganache (about a teaspoon) on top of the buttercream. Gently place the top shell onto the icing of the bum. Better do a quick taste test . . .

HAZELNUT MACARONS

TIMING

PREP 20 mins

BAKING 12–15 mins

ICING & DECORATING
10–20 mins

MAKES approx. 44
shells = 22 macarons

INGREDIENTS
Macaron shells

150 g (5½ oz) raw
hazelnuts

125 g (4½ oz) almond
meal

225 g (8 oz) icing
sugar

225 g (8 oz) caster
sugar

60 g (2¼ oz) water

2 x 83 g (3 oz) egg
white

Filling & decoration

1½ teaspoons
hazelnut oil (LorAnn)

1 recipe Swiss
Meringue
Buttercream
(page 104)

75 g (2½ oz) Dutch
cocoa

50 g (1¾ oz) Salted
Caramel (optional;
page 129)

100 g (3½ oz)
chopped dark
chocolate

*These are one of my favourite flavours of macaron, and
I had them as part of my wedding desserts; they hold a
special place in my memory bank.*

METHOD

Important note: Below I've given all the steps for making my Hazelnut
Macarons—if you've already made macarons lots of times, then this will
be all you'll need. However, if you're new to macaron making you'll need
to follow my step-by-step instructional (complete with excellent photos)
on pages 146–153. Also, have you read *Macarons According to Me* (pages
142–145) yet? If not, go do that now as it's important.

Preheat your oven to between 125°C and 135°C (260–275°F). Get all your
equipment and ingredients ready, and line your baking tray with pre-cut
non-stick baking paper laid over a macaron template.

Now, put your hazelnuts in your blender and blend until fine, making
sure you don't overblend or you will end up with hazelnut butter. The
chances are you won't get a consistently fine grind, but don't worry.
Transfer the ground hazelnuts to a sieve and use a spatula to push as
much through as you can. Put the nutty chunks back in the blender and
give them another whizz, then tip into the sieve and repeat the pushing
through. Weigh your sieved ground hazelnuts to make sure you have
100 g (3½ oz). Set any leftover crumbs aside.

Blend your almond meal and icing sugar on high until combined and the
almond meal is a bit finer. Put this in your mixing bowl, add your ground
hazelnuts and stir to just combine.

Start heating your combined caster sugar and water, and pop the
first 83 g (3 oz) of egg white in your mixer bowl fitted with the whisk
attachment. When the sugar syrup reaches about 115°C (240°F), start
your egg white whipping. Once your sugar syrup reaches 122°C (252°F),
slowly pour it down the side of the mixer bowl into the semi-whipped
egg white, keeping the mixer going the whole time. Keep it beating until
the bowl is cool and the meringue is good and stiff.

Meanwhile, start mixing the second 83 g (3 oz) of egg white into your
blended hazelnut/almond mixture until it resembles a thick paste that

Continued overleaf

you can roll into a ball and squish without cracks appearing. (Adjust as necessary with extra almond meal or egg white, but don't use too much.)

Add half the meringue to your macaronage, mixing with a smearing motion until it's a uniform consistency. Add the remaining meringue, and slowly and gently fold it in until you have a mixture with a perfect 'ribbon' consistency. Transfer to your piping bag with its nozzle, twist the end closed and start piping. When done, carefully remove the template and bang the tray on the benchtop several times to remove air bubbles.

Put the tray of macarons straight into the middle of your preheated oven and set your timer (I set mine for 14 mins; you may want to start at 12). Check that the feet are cooked properly; if not, cook for a minute longer and check again. When they're done, let them cool on the paper, then marry up perfectly matching pairs of shells. Lay them out in rows with one bum up, one top up.

When you have finished baking all of your macaron shells and they're cooling, crank your oven up to 180°C (350°F). Spread your leftover hazelnut crumbs over a baking tray and lightly roast for a few mins. Tip them out onto a plate to cool.

Add the hazelnut oil to your buttercream, and sift your cocoa into the bowl as well. Do NOT do this near any kind of airflow, like open windows, fans, etc.—you'll get covered in a liberal dusting of cocoa and will likely be picking it out of your nose for days. Mix, either by hand or using your mixer, until nicely combined.

Using a large French star tip for our signature macaron filling, pipe dollops onto your macaron bums. We like to add a dollop of our salted caramel on top of the buttercream, too.

In a suitable bowl (duh), melt your dark chocolate in the microwave in 30-second bursts, stirring after each burst. Spoon it into a new piping bag and snip the end off; you don't need a nozzle for this. Squirt some dollops of chocolate on the tops of each macaron, doing about four macarons at a time. Add a sprinkle of your roasted hazelnut crumb on top of the melted chocolate.

Once the chocolate is set, gently place the top shell onto the icing of the bum. Repeat until you've done them all, then quickly scoff one as a reward.

WATERMELON MACARONS

TIMING

PREP 20 mins

BAKING 24–30 mins

ICING & DECORATING 10–20 mins

MAKES approx. 44 shells = 22 macarons

INGREDIENTS

Macaron shells

225 g (8 oz) almond meal

225 g (8 oz) icing sugar

225 g (8 oz) caster sugar

60 g (2¼ oz) water

2 x 83 g (3 oz) egg white

1 teaspoon watermelon flavour (LorAnn)

½ teaspoon pink gel food colour

½ teaspoon green gel food colour

20 g (¾ oz) black chia seeds

Filling & decoration

1 recipe Vanilla Bean Swiss Meringue Buttercream (page 107)

METHOD

Important note: If you're experienced at making macarons, the steps below are all you'll need—you'll know how things should look. If you're new to this, you should really follow my step-by-step instructional (complete with awesome photos) on pages 146–153. Also, if you haven't yet read *Macarons According to Me* (pages 142–145), do that before you start.

Preheat your oven to between 125°C and 135°C (260–275°F). Get all your equipment and ingredients ready, and line two baking trays with pre-cut non-stick baking paper laid over a macaron template.

Blend your almond meal and icing sugar on high until they're combined and the almond meal is a bit finer.

Start heating the combined caster sugar and water, and put the first 83 g (3 oz) of egg white in your mixer bowl fitted with the whisk attachment. When the sugar syrup reaches about 115°C (240°F), start your egg white whipping. Once your sugar syrup reaches 122°C (252°F), slowly pour it down the side of the mixer bowl into the semi-whipped egg white, keeping the mixer going the whole time. Keep it beating until the bowl is cool and the meringue is nice and stiff.

Meanwhile, start mixing the second 83 g (3 oz) of egg white into your blended almond mixture, along with the watermelon flavour. Mix until it resembles a thick paste that you can roll into a ball and squish without cracks appearing. (Adjust as necessary with extra almond meal or egg white, just not too much of either.)

Using your scales, divide your macaronage evenly by weight into two bowls. Add pink food colour to one bowl and green to the other, and mix each until well combined and evenly coloured.

Now split your meringue in half by weight. Add half of one lot of meringue to your pink macaronage, mixing with a smearing motion until it's a uniform consistency. Add the rest of that meringue, and slowly and gently fold it in until you have a mixture with a perfect 'ribbon' consistency. Transfer to your piping bag with its nozzle, twist the end closed and start piping.

When you have your tray of pink macarons shells piped and ready to go in the oven (remember to remove the template and do the banging), sprinkle a small amount of chia seeds over your wet macarons. Put the tray straight into the middle of your preheated oven and set your timer (I set mine for 14 mins; you may want to start at 12). Check that the feet are cooked properly; if not, cook for a minute longer and check again. When they're done, let them cool on the paper.

While the pink shells are baking, add the remaining meringue, in two lots as before, to your green macaronage. Use a clean piping bag and nozzle to pipe the green shells, then carefully remove the template and bang the tray on the bench to remove any air bubbles. Once the pink shells are cooked, pop the green shells in the oven and bake them the same way.

Once all your macaron shells have cooled, marry up each pink top with a perfectly matching green bum. Line up the tops and bums for filling and decorating.

Using a large French star tip for our signature macaron filling, pipe dollops of buttercream onto your green macaron bums. Gently place each pink top onto the icing of the bum. And you're done.

FLAVOURED MACARON SUGGESTIONS

———

Now that you are the Karate Kid to my Mr Miyagi and you've macaroned on and macaroned off and achieved macaron success, try some of the following flavours. Take everything I have taught you and macaron to your heart's content. Don't forget to do your happy dance after each successful batch.

STRAWBERRY (PICTURED)
- Add ½ teaspoon of strawberry flavour to your macaronage and colour with gel colour as desired.
- Fill with Vanilla Bean Swiss Meringue Buttercream (page 107) and crushed freeze-dried strawberries.

LEMON
- Add ½ teaspoon of lemon flavour to your macaronage and colour with gel colour as desired.
- Fill with Lemon Cream Cheese Icing (page 112) and Lemon Curd (page 122).

VANILLA BEAN
- Add ½ teaspoon of vanilla bean paste and 1 teaspoon of vanilla extract to your macaronage.
- Fill with Salted Caramel Ganache (page 132) or Vanilla Bean Swiss Meringue Buttercream (page 107).

BLACK DORIS PLUM
- Add ½ teaspoon of vanilla bean paste and 1 teaspoon of vanilla extract to your macaronage, and colour it with plum gel colour.
- Put 100 g (3½ oz) canned Black Doris plums in a sieve and push through so there are no large chunks or stones. Add the sieved plums to Swiss Meringue Buttercream (page 104) and mix well to combine. Then fill your macarons.
- If you want a stronger plum taste, you can sprinkle crushed freeze-dried plums on top of the icing before putting the top shell on.

Continued overleaf

LEMON & LIME

- Follow the instructions for Watermelon Macarons (pages 168–169) for how to split-colour your macs. Add ¼ teaspoon of lemon oil and yellow gel colour to one half, and ¼ teaspoon of lime oil and green gel colour to the other half.
- Fill with Vanilla Bean Swiss Meringue Buttercream (page 107) and Citrus Curd (page 122).

COOKIES & CREAM (PICTURED)

- Add ½ teaspoon of vanilla bean paste and 1 teaspoon of vanilla extract to your macaronage.
- Fill with Cookies and Cream Swiss Meringue Buttercream (page 107).
- Chill the macarons. Melt 300 g (10½ oz) of dark chocolate, then dip half of each macaron sideways into the chocolate and sprinkle with crumbled Double Chocolate Cookies (page 191). Sit the macarons on their ends on baking paper for the chocolate to set.

PEACH

- Add 1 teaspoon of peach flavour to your macaronage.
- Prep your piping bag by painting three stripes of peach gel colour inside the bag, starting from the nozzle and going two-thirds of the way up the inside of the bag. Carefully fill the bag with macaron mixture and continue as normal. Your macarons will pipe with a peach-coloured swirl.
- Fill with Vanilla Bean Swiss Meringue Buttercream (page 107).

ORANGE SHERBET

- Add ½ teaspoon of orange oil and 1 teaspoon of orange gel food colour to the macaronage.
- Fill with Vanilla Bean Swiss Meringue Buttercream (page 107) and sprinkle generously with orange sherbet before putting on the tops.

COCONUT & LYCHEE

- Add 1 teaspoon of coconut essence to your macaronage.
- Fill with Vanilla Bean Swiss Meringue Buttercream (page 107) and a generous amount of crushed freeze-dried lychees.

BROWNIES
& COOKIES

BASIC BROWNIE

TIMING

PREP 20 mins

BAKING approx.
40 mins

MAKES 9 pieces

INGREDIENTS

220 g (7¾ oz) butter

60 g (2¼ oz) Dutch cocoa

5 eggs

400 g (14 oz) caster sugar

½ teaspoon vanilla extract

125 g (4½ oz) plain flour

200 g (7 oz) chopped 70% dark chocolate

icing sugar, to dust

You can bake this as is and it will be epic, but if you want it to be extra, check out the brownie variations overleaf. The one in the photo opposite is my S'mores Brownie.

METHOD

Preheat your oven to 170°C (325°F). Prep a 20 cm (8 in) square baking tin with baking spray and line it with baking paper.

Put the butter in suitable bowl and microwave it in bursts of 10–20 seconds, until melted. Transfer it to the bowl of your stand mixer along with the cocoa and mix these together by hand using a spatula, until just combined. Then start whisking on high speed.

Crack your eggs into the bowl you used for the butter—this will allow you to slop them into the mixer while it is running without the stress of dropping a whole egg in, shell and all, and destroying the whole mix (yes, I'm speaking from experience).

Add the eggs from your bowl one at a time to your mixer, allowing them to whip and incorporate after each addition. When they have all been added, keep whipping for a further 5 mins *at least!* The mixture should double in size. Stop the mixer and add your sugar and vanilla, then whip for another 5 mins.

Now add your flour and chocolate and fold them in by hand until just combined. Tip the mixture into your baking tin and bake for about 40 mins. Remove from the oven when the outside of the brownie is solid but the middle is still jubbly—I realise this is a random description, so I thought I would enlighten y'all on the meaning via Google. First hit was this: 'adjective. informal. Of the stomach, bottom, etc.: plump, fleshy. Hence, of a woman: having large breasts.' Well shit, I couldn't have put it better myself, Oxford Dictionary!! So when I say jubbly, what I mean is a combination of jiggly and wobbly. This 'jubbliness' will mean your brownie will be dense and chewy and gooey once cooled (in the tin). This cuts the best if it's chilled for a few hours. Once your brownie is cooled, remove it from the tin and cut it into 9 pieces—that's 3 by 3—and sprinkle with a dusting of icing sugar. It's a bloody good time.

FLAVOUR INSPO FOR BROWNIES

___

S'MORES BROWNIE

Note that this recipe uses several items from other recipes within the book, so make sure you prep them ahead.

1 recipe Basic Brownie (page 176)
100 g (3½ oz) broken-up Graham Crackers dough (page 195)
8–10 Vanilla Bean Marshmallows (page 217)
Salted Caramel (page 129), to drizzle

Follow the method for the basic recipe, but before you pour your mixture into the tin, spread the bottom of the tin with the broken pieces of Graham Crackers dough. Arrange the marshmallows on top of the mixture just before putting it in the oven—these will melt and caramelise over the top of the brownie as it bakes. Before serving, drizzle with a generous helping of salted caramel.

ESPRESSO WALNUT BROWNIE

1 recipe Basic Brownie (page 176)
30 ml (1 fl oz) espresso, or 1 tablespoon instant coffee dissolved in 30 ml (1 fl oz) hot water
150 g (5½ oz) walnuts
Salted Caramel (page 129), to drizzle

Follow the method for the basic recipe, but add your coffee to the butter and cocoa mixture and stir it in before adding the eggs. Once your brownie mixture is in the tin, top it with walnuts, distributing them evenly. Bake for 40–50 mins until jubbly. Before serving, load up with a good drizzle of salted caramel.

BERRY BROWNIE

1 recipe Basic Brownie (page 176)
200 g (7 oz) frozen berries
icing sugar, to dust
10 g (¼ oz) freeze-dried berries

Follow the method as per the basic recipe. Pour the mix into the tin, then top it with frozen berries, distributing them evenly. Bake for 40–50 mins until jubbly. Before serving, dust with a generous sprinkling of icing sugar and sprinkle with some crushed freeze-dried berries.

ALLERGY-FRIENDLY CHICKPEA BROWNIE

FREE FROM GLUTEN, EGGS, DAIRY AND ANIMAL PRODUCTS

TIMING

PREP 25 mins

BAKING approx. 45 mins

MAKES 9 pieces

INGREDIENTS

400 g (14 oz) can chickpeas

125 g (4½ oz) coconut milk

125 g (4½ oz) dairy-free butter substitute

1 teaspoon vanilla extract

200 g (7 oz) soft brown sugar

60 g (2¼ oz) almond meal

60 g (2¼ oz) Dutch cocoa

½ teaspoon baking powder

100 g (3½ oz) gluten-free flour

150 g (5½ oz) chopped 70% dark chocolate, plus extra for topping

Dutch cocoa or icing sugar, to dust

I love this brownie, not just because it's tasty as fuck while allowing so many people with aversions and allergies to delight in our talent, but also because it actually came about out of my inability to eat another mouthful of hummus. Do you know Bruce? He went and invented aquafaba (see page 26), which if you didn't know is bean brine (most commonly chickpea brine). Bruce is the Messiah—ask his friends, they will tell you. Thanks to Bruce we were buying in 2.5 kg cans of chickpeas just to get the brine for our allergy-friendly baking. I didn't want to waste all those chickpeas so I was making roasted chickpeas, chickpea patties and lots of fucken HUMMUS! It got ridiculous, and I was starting to really dislike the chickpea (which is unfortunate as it's a staple of my vegetarian diet). So I created this brownie recipe specifically to use up the leftover chickpeas. Bruce has a lot to answer for. Everyone say, 'Thank you, Bruce.'

METHOD

Preheat your oven to 160°C (315°F). Prep an 18 cm (7 in) square baking tin with baking spray and line it with baking paper.

Drain your chickpeas. KEEP THE BRINE FOR BRUCE. Put the drained chickpeas and coconut milk in your blender and blend until you have a smooth paste.

While this is blending, put your dairy-free butter, vanilla and sugar in the bowl of your stand mixer fitted with the paddle attachment and beat until light and fluffy. Add the chickpea paste mixture and beat to combine.

Add the remaining ingredients except the chocolate, and slowly beat until just combined. Add the chocolate and fold it through by hand. Dump the mixture into your prepared tin and evenly sprinkle a handful of chocolate over the top. This can now be baked as is, or you can try one of our flavour alternatives listed overleaf.

Continued overleaf

Bake for about 45 mins—you want the outer edges to be solid and the inner bit to be slightly soft. Allow to cool in the tin, then chill in the fridge for an hour before cutting. Sprinkle with a dusting of Dutch cocoa or icing sugar before serving.

FLAVOUR INSPO FOR ALLERGY-FRIENDLY BROWNIES

———

RASPBERRY
150 g (5½ oz) frozen raspberries
10 g (¼ oz) freeze-dried raspberries

Distribute the frozen berries over the top of the brownie mixture before putting it in the oven, pressing the berries slightly into the mixture. When serving, crush some freeze-dried raspberries over each brownie.

WALNUT & CARAMEL (PICTURED)
150 g (5½ oz) walnuts
Allergy-friendly Salted Caramel (page 131), to drizzle

Distribute the walnuts over the top of the brownie mixture before putting it in the oven, pressing them firmly into the mixture. Once cooled, drizzle liberally with the caramel.

STRAWBERRY WHITE CHOCOLATE COOKIES

TIMING

DOUGH PREP 20 mins

CHILLING/RESTING
1 hour minimum,
preferably overnight

BAKING approx.
15 mins

MAKES 15 cookies

INGREDIENTS

50 g (1¾ oz) rolled
oats

50 g (1¾ oz) almond
meal

125 g (4½ oz) plain
flour

½ teaspoon baking
soda

½ teaspoon baking
powder

¼ teaspoon salt

150 g (5½ oz) butter,
at room temperature

200 g (7 oz) soft
brown sugar

1 egg

½ teaspoon vanilla
extract

½ teaspoon
strawberry flavour

170 g (6 oz) white
chocolate buttons

15 g (½ oz) freeze-
dried strawberries

METHOD

Put your oats in a blender and blend until fine. Add the almond meal, flour, baking soda, baking powder and salt, and pulse to combine.

In the bowl (ideally) of your stand mixer fitted with the paddle attachment, cream together your butter and sugar until light and fluffy. (You can do this by hand or with a hand-held beater if you must.) Add the egg, vanilla and strawberry flavour, then beat to combine.

Add the dry ingredients from your blender, along with the chocolate buttons, and fold together until just combined.

Scoop portions of dough onto a tray lined with baking paper (we use a cookie scoop but you don't have to; a tablespoon will do.) You can space them close together, as this is just the chilling stage. Chill for at least an hour in the fridge (or less in the freezer), until the dough is firm and holds its shape. If you want, you can now put them into a container and store in the freezer to bake as required.

When you do bake them, preheat your oven to 160°C (315°F).

Line a baking tray with baking paper and put your chilled cookies onto the tray, leaving a GENEROUS SPACE between them as they will spread a lot. Bake for 12–15 mins, or until golden but slightly underdone in the middle. Make sure you stick to this bit, because they really do need to be slightly crispy around the outside and chewy in the centre.

Allow to cool on the tray, crushing a few freeze-dried strawberries over them to give them an extra pop of colour.

ALLERGY-FRIENDLY DOUBLE CHOCOLATE COOKIES

FREE FROM GLUTEN, EGGS, DAIRY AND ANIMAL PRODUCTS

TIMING

DOUGH PREP 20 mins

CHILLING/RESTING
2 hours minimum, preferably overnight

BAKING approx. 15 mins

MAKES 20 cookies (10 sandwiches)

INGREDIENTS

75 g (2½ oz) almond meal

225 g (8 oz) gluten-free flour

170 g (6 oz) soft brown sugar

40 g (1½ oz) Dutch cocoa

175 g (6 oz) dairy-free butter substitute

75 g (2½ oz) golden syrup

100 g (3½ oz) boiling water

1½ teaspoons baking soda

125 g (4½ oz) 70% dark chocolate chunks

Allergy-friendly Strawberry & Nutmeg Ice Cream (optional; page 236)

METHOD

Put the almond meal, flour, sugar and cocoa into the bowl of your stand mixer fitted with the paddle attachment, and mix on low to combine.

On the stove, heat the dairy-free butter and golden syrup in a pot until the butter has melted. Separately, mix the boiling water and baking soda together and add it to the pot, stirring to combine.

Add this liquid mixture to your dry ingredients and mix on low until combined. Add the chocolate and fold through by hand. Chill the mixture in the fridge for 1 hour before scooping.

Scoop portions of mixture (using a cookie scoop, if you have one) onto a tray lined with baking paper. You can space them close together, as this is just the chilling stage. Chill for at least an hour in the fridge (or less time in the freezer), so that the dough is firm and holds its shape. At this point you can put the raw cookies into a container and store them in the freezer. If you do this, make sure you layer them between pieces of baking paper as this recipe is stickier than the other cookie recipes and you can learn from my mistakes. If you don't, trust me they will all freeze together and you will be carving them apart and that is not a good time.

When ready to bake, preheat your oven to 170°C (325°F).

Line a baking tray with baking paper and put your chilled cookies onto the tray, leaving LOTS OF SPACE between them as they will spread. Bake for about 15 mins or until they are crispy around the edges, then remove from the oven and allow to cool on the tray.

I love these sandwiched together with a generous helping of our Allergy-friendly Strawberry & Nutmeg Ice Cream.

ALLERGY-FRIENDLY COOKIE SANDWICHES

TIMING

DOUGH PREP 20–30 mins

CHILLING/RESTING 1 hour minimum, preferably overnight

BAKING approx. 15 mins

MAKES 15 cookie sandwiches

INGREDIENTS

300 g (10½ oz) cashew pulp (leftover pulp from making cashew milk, see page 243)

200 g (7 oz) gluten-free flour

1 tablespoon salt flakes

150 g (5½ oz) coconut sugar

100 g (3½ oz) coconut oil, melted but coolish

150 g (5½ oz) chopped 70% dark chocolate

400 g (14 oz) Allergy-friendly Chocolate Ganache (page 116), ratio 1:1

This is another recipe that was developed out of my unwillingness to waste. If I'm going to the trouble of buying cashews to make milk from, I don't JUST want to milk them—I WANT TO MILK THEM FOR ALL THEY'RE WORTH. So in this recipe, cashews have become the hero as a cookie base post-milking. These cookies are seriously addictive and probably the healthiest thing I've created to date.

METHOD

Chuck all the ingredients except the chocolate and ganache in the bowl of your stand mixer fitted with the paddle attachment, and mix on low to combine. Add the chocolate and mix until just combined. Make sure that your coconut oil is only just melted and not hot, or it will melt the chocolate. If this does happen, don't stress—the cookies will still work and be delicious, it's just not what I intended for them.

Scoop out portions of mixture using a small cookie scoop (about the size of a tablespoon)—if you don't have one, just use whatever you can. You just need the cookies to be fairly evenly sized so that they don't make wonky, misshapen sandwiches. If you are winging it without a cookie scoop, roll the portions into balls and place on a tray lined with baking paper, leaving about 2 cm (¾ in) space between balls. If you're scooping with a scoop, just scoop onto the tray, spaced out.

When the tray is full, lay another layer of baking paper over the top. Grab a second tray and use it to evenly squish the cookie dough until it is about 1.5 cm (⅝ in) thick. Chill for at least an hour in the fridge (or less in the freezer), so that the dough is firm and holds its shape. You can put the raw cookies into a container at this stage and store in the freezer to bake as required.

Whenever you decide to bake them, preheat your oven to 180°C (350°F). Line a baking tray with baking paper and put the chilled cookies onto the tray, leaving a small space between each cookie. These don't spread so the gap doesn't have to be enormous.

Continued overleaf

Bake for 15 mins, or until golden and crispy around the edges. Allow to cool on the tray before icing.

While you're waiting for your cookies to bake and cool, prep your ganache. Put it into a piping bag while it is still a squirty consistency. When the cookies are cool, snip about ½ cm (¼ in) off the tip of the bag.

Marry up your cookies so that each sandwich-to-be has a top and a bum. Set them out on your tray with one cookie facing up and the other facing down. Squirt the ganache in zig-zags over the tops, and squeeze a generous dollop on the bums. Sandwich the tops and bums together and allow the ganache to set.

GRAHAM CRACKERS

TIMING

PREP 30 mins

CHILLING 15 mins

BAKING approx.
15 mins

MAKES approx. 30
crackers

INGREDIENTS

220 g (7¾ oz) plain
flour

150 g (5½ oz)
wholemeal flour

50 g (1¾ oz) bran

½ teaspoon salt
flakes

1 teaspoon baking
soda

2 teaspoons ground
cinnamon

250 g (9 oz) butter

150 g (5½ oz) soft
brown sugar

40 g (1½ oz) golden
syrup

How did these even come to be? I created these one day because I'd heard about graham crackers on just about every dang American movie and always wondered what was so special about these crackers and why were people putting crackers with marshmallow and chocolate? I mean, crackers are for cheese, right? If it's sweet it's a biscuit, right? Consider me confused! After doing some research, I soon realised that America's cracker is very different to a New Zealand cracker.

Once I knew what a graham cracker was, I created my own so I could make a gourmet version of S'mores (see page 228). I didn't have any intention of selling the graham crackers, to be honest, but when I added Salted Caramel (see page 129) to my market menu I didn't want to have people trying it on a stick. So I baked up some graham crackers and broke them into pieces so that people at the markets had a vehicle for tasting my epic caramel. I swear the whole market was filled with moans and groans over how delicious these crackers and caramel were. People were loving the caramel and it was flying off the shelf, but ALSO people were asking where they could buy the crackers. I was kicking myself because of course I had only made them as tasters for caramel. So I told everyone that at the next market we would have the crackers for sale by themselves.

These crackers have been given multiple seals of approval by Americans and Canadians who say they are better than the real thing. They are so moreish and I am guilty of having them for breakfast. They are perfect with a cup of tea before bed, or as a vehicle for salted caramel (much more dignified than eating it with a spoon), or crumbled over ice cream, or used in a cheesecake base. Don't forget the S'mores, though—they're the best application for these crackers!

Continued overleaf

METHOD

Combine the dry ingredients in a bowl, mix together and set aside.

Put the butter, sugar and golden syrup in the bowl of your stand mixer fitted with the beater attachment and beat BEAT BEAT. (You know the drill—I'm over here sniggering as per usual. Think 'beat the meat', but with butter.) You want to beat it until it becomes pale and fluffy. Stop and scrape down the mixer bowl a couple of times to ensure all the butter has been combined.

Add the dry ingredients to your mixer bowl and mix on low until the mixture forms a soft dough.

Divide your dough into two, and get two pieces of baking paper about the same size as your baking trays. Roll out your graham cracker dough between the two pieces of paper until it's about ¼ cm (⅛ in) thick. Try to roll it out into a generally rectangular shape, as this will maximise the number of crackers you'll get.

Peel off the top piece of paper. Using a ruler and a wiggly pastry wheel*, score the dough into crackers measuring 7.5 x 5 cm (3 x 2 in). Prick each cracker twice with a fork. Repeat with the remaining dough.

Put the trays of crackers in your fridge to chill for about 15 mins, or in the freezer for 10 mins because that is way faster and it's what I do. While the dough is chilling, preheat your oven to 160°C (315°F).

Once your dough is chilled, carefully break the crackers apart. Keep the funny-shaped outer bits in your freezer for making the S'mores Brownie (page 178)!

Lay your chilled crackers on a baking tray lined with baking paper, leaving a finger-width gap between each cracker. These don't spread, so don't fret about the spacing. Bake for about 15 mins until golden with a slight crisp around the edge. Remove from the oven and allow to cool on the tray. Store in an airtight container.

* I made up this tool name—I actually have no idea of its technical term, but you can see what I'm talking about in the tools section. It's the tool with the red handle that looks like a cock and balls. When we were photographing the tools, Lottie (talented camera-wielding artist) was hovering on a stool to get that awesome bird's-eye-view type photo, and said we should turn the wiggly pastry wheel up the other way 'cause it looked like a cock. This of course made me determined to leave it as is, looking all cock-like 'cause YOU KNOW ME, I do love a classic cock-and-balls laugh.

SWEET
TREATS &
DRINKS

—

CLASSIC RUSSIAN FUDGE

TIMING

PREP 5 mins

COOKING approx. 40 mins

SETTING approx. 2 hours

MAKES 64 pieces

INGREDIENTS

1 kg (2 lb 4 oz) caster sugar

155 g (5½ oz) butter

70 g (2½ oz) golden syrup

155 g (5½ oz) milk

1 teaspoon salt

250 g (9 oz) sweetened condensed milk

1 teaspoon vanilla essence

Oh Russian fudge, I truly have you to thank for where I am today—you are my OG MO-FO kitchen homie. The fudge pot used to come out just for work shouts and Christmas gifts— now we have multiple fudge pots, multiple flavours, custom-printed boxes and customers worldwide who hungus it.

I swear that this fudge is everything you remember from your home-baking activities at your grandparents' house. Remember eagerly waiting for it to set so you could scoff it in front of the TV until the Goodnight Kiwi told you it was bedtime? It really does hold all those delicious memories in every bite. It has that traditional old-fashioned, crumbly, melt-in-your-mouth texture. What memories will this evoke? What memories will you guys be making with your friends and families?

METHOD

Prep a 20 cm (8 in) square tin by lightly spraying it with cooking spray and lining it with baking paper.

Put all the ingredients except the vanilla in a large pot. Heat on low, stirring occasionally. The mixture will melt together and then start to slowly boil with large, rolling, popping bubbles. Be careful when you stir it, as these bubbles can pop and splash you—and trust me, that is not ideal and burns instantly. (Once it splashed on my cheek and I instantly had an ugly blister, and so many hand and arm burns have been caused by delicious Russian fudge. SO BE FUCKEN WARNED.)

Grab a digital thermometer and set it to alarm at 118°C (244°F). For years, I did the soft-ball test even when I was supplying stores and selling at markets—I was stubborn, and didn't want to let go of the method I had grown up using. But seriously, this book is filled with recipes that require a digital thermometer so just do yourself a favour and get one. Stick the thermometer in the fudge pot, and when the alarm goes off, remove your fudge from the heat and add the vanilla.

NOW FOR THE ALL-IMPORTANT SECRET: use an electric hand-held beater. In my opinion, not knowing this tip is hands down the reason why so many people fail at fudge. I always hear 'I just can't get

Continued overleaf

it to set', and I know why instantly! It's something I struggled with in my early days of fudge making until my laziness got the better of me and I grabbed an electric beater to do the job most cookbooks told me I should do by hand. The electric beater will aerate and cool your fudge so that when it sets it sets hard, but when bitten into, it melts in your mouth. So—using an electric hand-held beater fitted with whisk attachments—whisk the fudge on low to start with, then increase the speed as the fudge thickens and splashes less.

You will know your fudge is ready when it is thick and you see lines forming in the mixture. Also, the centre pole on the whisk attachment will have a build-up of fudge that is all spikey. THESE VISUAL CUES ARE IMPERATIVE TO SUCCESS. (You only need ask my bestest friend Rose, who I taught years ago to make my Russian fudge. Other than my staff, Rose is the only person I have ever shared my Russian fudge techniques with. She made it for other expats in Singapore when her husband Dean was posted there with the Navy, and I believe it even shows up at her kids' bake sales. Needless to say, my Russian fudge has made Rose far more popular than she would have been otherwise. You're welcome, Rose, I love you epic amounts and thank you for always being so pretty. I can't wait to see how popular it makes everyone else, too.)

Once your fudge is showing these visual cues, pour it into your prepared tin and smooth it out with a non-stick spatula. Allow to set for about 30 mins, then use a sharp knife to pre-cut the fudge into 8 squares x 8 squares. Allow to completely set hard at room temp, then remove from the tin and break into pieces. You will know you have made Magnolia Kitchen-worthy fudge if your fudge meets these requirements:

- When you taste-test a piece of fudge, bite a corner off your square. If you see teeth marks dragging down the side of the fudge, this is indicator of success number one.
- When you have a piece of Russian fudge in your mouth, use your tongue to crush it against the roof of your mouth—move your tongue from side to side, really crushing that fudge. If it feels like the inside of your mouth has just been licked by a cat, then you have failed— go straight to jail and do not pass go. If an overwhelming sense of joy floods your taste buds, making them sing, this is your second indicator of success and I salute you (but really I'm saluting myself, because this recipe is awesome and so am I).

Store in an airtight container. This will last months if kept at a neutral temperature out of direct sunlight. But let's be honest, what kind of person are you if you have fudge in your pantry for months?

OPPOSITE Boxes of fudge and other deliciousness on the shelves at Magnolia Kitchen Sweet Cafe. The hand-painted logo on the wall was my market signage at the very first 'Treat Shop'. It has pride of place in the cafe as a reminder of how far I've come.

DARK CHOCOLATE FUDGE

TIMING

PREP 5 mins

COOKING approx. 40 mins

SETTING approx. 2 hours

MAKES 64 pieces

INGREDIENTS

800 g (1 lb 12 oz) caster sugar

125 g (4½ oz) butter

125 g (4½ oz) milk

½ teaspoon salt

200 g (7 oz) sweetened condensed milk

200 g (7 oz) chopped 70% dark chocolate

METHOD

Important note: There are some visual cues you will need to know about before clocking fudge—do yourself a favour and study the Russian fudge recipe on page 202 before turning that stove on!

Prep a 20 cm (8 in) square tin with a light spray of cooking spray and a lining of baking paper. Put all the ingredients except the dark chocolate in a large pot. Heat on low, stirring occasionally. The mixture will melt together and then start to slowly boil with large, rolling, popping bubbles. Be careful when you stir it, as these bubbles can pop and splash you and it WILL result in a burn. Trust me.

Set a digital thermometer to alarm at 118°C (244°F) and stick it in your fudge. When the fudge reaches that temperature, remove from the heat and add the chocolate. Using an electric hand-held beater with whisk attachments, whisk the fudge on low to start with until the chocolate is melted, then increase the speed as the fudge thickens and splashes less.

You will know your fudge is ready when it is thick and you see lines forming in the mixture. Also, the centre pole on the whisk attachments will have a build-up of fudge that is all spikey. THESE VISUAL CUES ARE IMPERATIVE TO SUCCESS. Once your fudge is showing these visual cues, pour it into your prepared tin and smooth it out with a non-stick spatula. Allow to set for about 30 mins, then use a sharp knife to pre-cut the fudge into 8 squares x 8 squares. Allow to completely set hard at room temp, then remove from the tin and break into pieces. Store in an airtight container.

FLAVOUR INSPO FOR DARK CHOCOLATE FUDGE

CHILLI DARK CHOCOLATE FUDGE

Add 1–2 teaspoons of chilli powder with the chopped chocolate.

ESPRESSO DARK CHOCOLATE FUDGE

Add 3 tablespoons Kahlúa and 60 g (2¼ oz) powdered instant coffee to your pot at the beginning.

RASPBERRY WHITE CHOCOLATE FUDGE

TIMING

PREP 5 mins

COOKING approx. 40 mins

SETTING approx. 2 hours

MAKES 64 pieces

INGREDIENTS

800 g (1 lb 12 oz) caster sugar

125 g (4½ oz) butter

125 g (4½ oz) milk

½ teaspoon salt

200 g (7 oz) sweetened condensed milk

200 g (7 oz) chopped white chocolate

20 g (¾ oz) freeze-dried raspberries, plus extra to sprinkle

METHOD

Important note: Fudge making is for the masters and you gotta know that without my all-important visual cues you will not succeed—so go and read the Russian fudge recipe on page 202 before you start.

Prep a 20 cm (8 in) square tin by lightly spraying with cooking spray and lining with baking paper.

Put all the ingredients except the white chocolate and raspberries* in a large pot. Heat on low, stirring occasionally; the mixture will melt together and then start to slowly boil with large, rolling, popping bubbles. At this stage be careful when you stir it, as these bubbles can pop and splash you, and it will instantly result in a burn. Be warned.

Get your digital thermometer and set it to alarm at 118°C (244°F), then put it in the fudge pot. When your fudge reaches that temperature, remove it from the heat and add the white chocolate. Using an electric hand-held beater with whisk attachments, whisk the fudge on low to start with until the white chocolate has melted. Increase the speed as the fudge thickens and splashes less.

Your fudge will be ready when it is thick and you see lines forming in the mixture. The centre pole on the whisk attachments will also have a build-up of fudge that is all spikey. THESE VISUAL CUES ARE IMPERATIVE TO SUCCESS. Once your fudge is showing these visual cues, add your freeze-dried raspberries and mix through with a non-stick spatula.

Pour into your prepared tin and smooth out with your spatula. Crush the extra freeze-dried raspberries, sprinkle over the top and push down with the spatula. Allow to set for about 30 mins, then use a sharp knife to pre-cut the fudge into 8 squares x 8 squares. Allow to completely set hard at room temp, then remove from the tin and break into pieces.

Store in an airtight container. This could last months if kept at a neutral temperature out of direct sunlight.

*For a nutty version, replace the raspberries with 100 g (3½ oz) roughly chopped macadamia nuts.

ALLERGY-FRIENDLY SALTED CARAMEL CASHEW FUDGE

TIMING

PREP overnight soaking + 30 mins

COOKING 40–60 mins

SETTING approx. 2 hours

MAKES 64 pieces

INGREDIENTS

Date Sauce

85 g (3 oz) pitted dates

125 g (4½ oz) boiling water

Cashew Milk

85 g (3 oz) raw cashews

hot water to cover

300 g (10½ oz) cold water

Cashew Butter

75 g (2½ oz) coconut oil

125 g (4½ oz) raw cashews

Fudge

250 g (9 oz) fresh cashew milk (see above)

100 g (3½ oz) date sauce (see above)

200 g (7 oz) cashew butter (see above)

½ teaspoon salt

1 kg (2 lb 4 oz) caster sugar

100 g (3½ oz) roasted cashews

2 teaspoons salt flakes

METHOD

Important note: Fudge has key visual cues that are imperative to making it successfully—before you start this recipe, go and read the Russian fudge method on page 202.

Put the dates in a heatproof bowl and cover with the boiling water. Cover the bowl and leave to soak overnight. Make the cashew milk following the method on page 243 (but without the vanilla), soaking the nuts overnight so that your cashew milk is made fresh in the morning.

Prep a 20 cm (8 in) square tin with a light spray of cooking spray and a lining of baking paper. Blend the dates and water until you get a smooth date sauce. For the cashew butter, melt the coconut oil and blend with the cashews until buttery-smooth.

To make the fudge, put all the ingredients except the roasted cashews and salt flakes in a large pot. Heat on low, stirring occasionally. The mixture will melt together, then start to slowly boil with large, rolling, popping bubbles— at this point, increase the heat to medium. Be careful when you stir it, as these bubbles can pop and splash you and immediately result in a BURN.

Set a digital thermometer to alarm at 118°C (244°F) and put it in your fudge pot. When the fudge reaches that temperature, remove from the heat. Using an electric hand-held beater with whisk attachments, whisk the fudge on low to start with, then increase the speed as it thickens and splashes less.

You will know your fudge is ready when it is thick and you see lines forming in the mixture. The centre pole on the whisk attachments will also have a build-up of fudge that is all spikey. THESE VISUAL CUES ARE IMPERATIVE TO SUCCESS. Once your fudge is showing these visual cues, add your roasted cashews and 1 teaspoon of salt flakes. Mix through using a non-stick spatula. Pour into your prepared tin and smooth out with the spatula. Sprinkle the remaining teaspoon of salt flakes over the top and push down with the spatula. Allow to set for about 30 mins, then use a sharp knife to pre-cut the fudge into 8 squares x 8 squares. Allow to completely set hard at room temp, then remove from the tin and break into pieces. Store in an airtight container.

GOURMET WHITE CHOCOLATE ROCKY ROAD

TIMING

PREP 30 mins (with marshmallows already made)

SETTING approx. 1 hour

MAKES 64 pieces

INGREDIENTS

600 g (1 lb 5 oz) white chocolate*

200 g (7 oz) Vanilla Bean Marshmallows (page 217)

75 g (2½ oz) desiccated coconut

140 g (5 oz) shelled pistachios

130 g (4½ oz) dried cranberries

METHOD

Prep a 20 cm (8 in) square tin by lightly spraying with cooking spray and lining with baking paper.

Put the chocolate in a microwave-safe bowl big enough to hold all the ingredients, and melt the chocolate in the microwave in 30-second bursts, stirring after each burst. Add all the other ingredients and stir to combine.

Tip into the prepared tin, push it around and make it as even as possible with a spatula, then allow to set. Using a sharp knife, cut into approx. 2.5 cm (1 in) square pieces. This is a pain in the arse to cut so be aware that it will look rustic, but that is part of the beauty of it. I love this one for Christmas because of the red and green that pops through. Store in an airtight container.

*For a dark chocolate version, replace the white chocolate with the same quantity of dark chocolate, and replace the coconut, pistachios and cranberries with 140 g (5 oz) roasted gourmet nuts and 20 g (¾ oz) freeze-dried cherries. It also looks great if you colour the Vanilla Bean Marshmallows pink.

VANILLA BEAN MARSHMALLOWS

TIMING

PREP 5 mins

COOKING AND MIXING approx. 40 mins

SETTING 4–6 hours, ideally overnight

MAKES 64 pieces

INGREDIENTS

125 g (4½ oz) water minus 1 tablespoon

20 g (¾ oz) powdered gelatine

2 x 85 g (3 oz) glucose

170 g (5¾ oz) caster sugar

62 g (2¼ oz) water

½ teaspoon salt

1 teaspoon vanilla extract

¼ teaspoon good-quality vanilla bean paste

50 g (1¾ oz) cornflour

50 g (1¾ oz) icing sugar

METHOD

Prep a 20 cm (8 in) square tin by spraying with cooking spray; set aside.

Combine the first lot of water and the gelatine in a microwave-safe bowl, and set aside to bloom.

Combine the first 85 g (3 oz) glucose with the sugar, second lot of water and salt in a pot and bring to the boil over a medium heat. Set your digital thermometer to alarm at 122°C (252°F) and put it in the pot. When the sugar syrup reaches about 115°C (239°F), heat the bloomed gelatine in the microwave for 2 mins or until the gelatine melts and becomes liquid.

Place the remaining 85 g (3 oz) glucose in the bowl of your stand mixer fitted with the whisk attachment, add the liquid gelatine and start mixing on low.

When your sugar syrup reaches 122°C (252°F), slowly pour it into the mixer, being careful to pour it down the side of the bowl not directly onto the whisk. Cover the mixer with a clean tea towel and turn to high speed for 10–12 mins—the bowl should become lukewarm to the touch.

Stop the mixer, add the vanillas and/or any other flavours and colours (see overleaf) and turn back onto high speed to combine. Scrape the marshmallow into your prepared tin and smooth with a non-stick spatula.

You know you want to lick that bowl . . . go on, DO IT.

Allow at least 4–6 hours for the marshmallow to set; overnight is best.

Sift the cornflour and icing sugar together into a large container. This is your dusting mix. Dust your bench with a little dusting mix, then remove the marshmallow slab from the tin and dust that too. Cut the marshmallow into 8 squares x 8 squares. Put these back in your large container, put the lid on and give it a vigorous *shake shake shake*—this will coat all the marshmallows and keep them from sticking together.

Store in an airtight container—they will keep for at least 2 months.

FLAVOUR INSPO FOR MARSHMALLOWS

PINEAPPLE LUMP MARSHMALLOWS (PICTURED)

After your marshmallow has whipped for 10–12 mins, stop the mixer and add 1 teaspoon yellow gel colour and ¼ teaspoon pineapple flavour (LorAnn). Mix on high for a further 2 mins to combine. Add ½ cup of small chocolate chips and fold through using a non-stick spatula. Once the mixture is in the tin and smoothed out, sprinkle more chocolate on top.

STRAWBERRY MARSHMALLOWS

After the marshmallow has whipped for 10–12 mins, stop the mixer and add ½ teaspoon pink gel colour, ½ teaspoon strawberry flavour (LorAnn) and 10 g (¼ oz) roughly crushed freeze-dried strawberry slices. Mix on high for 2 mins to combine. Once the mixture is in the tin and smoothed out, crush more freeze-dried strawberries on top.

MARBLED MARSHMALLOWS

Separate off about 1 cup of marshmallow mixture, add your desired marble colour to this portion and mix until completely coloured. Put the coloured marshmallow back into the mixture and fold gently until the desired marbled effect is achieved.

FAIRY BREAD MARSHMALLOWS

Use the basic vanilla bean recipe. Spread half the mixture into your tin, sprinkle generously with hundreds and thousands, then cover with the remaining mixture.

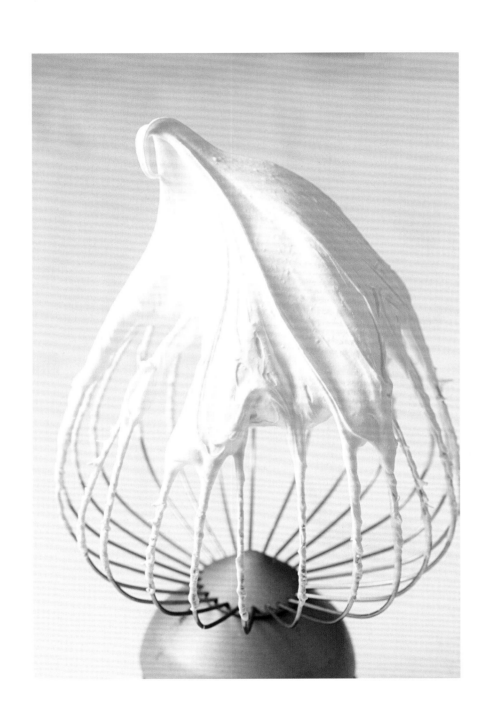

BASIC MERINGUE

INGREDIENTS

100 g (3½ oz) egg white

200 g (7 oz) caster sugar

METHOD

Put the egg white and sugar in a heatproof bowl (I do this in my metal stand mixer bowl). Grab a pot that is smaller than your bowl. Fill the pot halfway with water, bring it to the boil then turn down to a simmer.

Rest your bowl on top of the pot, and put a large spoon in the pot so that the steam can escape between the bowl and the pot. Stir the meringue-to-be until the sugar has dissolved into the egg white. To test this, dunk your thumb and pointer finger in and rub them together (this is gross and feels like snot, but it's the best way to test). You shouldn't feel any gritty bits of sugar.

Once the sugar is dissolved, transfer to your stand mixer bowl (if you're not already using it). Using the whisk attachment, mix on high until stiff peaks are achieved, like super-stiff. You want the bowl to have cooled and your meringue to be super-stiff—did I mention you want them stiff?!

Decide what you want to do with your meringue—Giant Meringues, Meringue Kisses, Meringue Mushrooms (these are cute as fuck)—and see the next recipes for how to make them.

MERINGUE KISSES

TIMING

PREP approx. 15 mins (with meringue already made)

BAKING 1–2 hours

MAKES approx. 20

INGREDIENTS

gel colour

½ teaspoon flavour oil (LorAnn) or 2 teaspoons fruit powder

1 recipe Basic Meringue (page 221)

METHOD

Preheat your oven to 90°C (195°F) and prep a baking tray with pre-cut baking paper.

Prep your piping bag with a large circular nozzle. Using a paintbrush, paint your gel colour inside the bag. Paint three stripes in various places, starting from inside the nozzle and going about two-thirds of the way up the piping bag.

Fold your flavour through your meringue, and carefully fill your piping bag with meringue. Use a small blob of meringue under each corner of your baking paper to stick it to the baking tray.

Now pipe large dollops of meringue: squeeze your piping bag close to the paper and keep squeezing as you pull up, then release the pressure and keep pulling up to create a little tail.

Bake the kisses for 1–2 hours—they will be done when the meringues come away cleanly from the baking paper. Remove from the oven and allow to cool.

Store in an airtight container, where they will keep for 7–10 days.

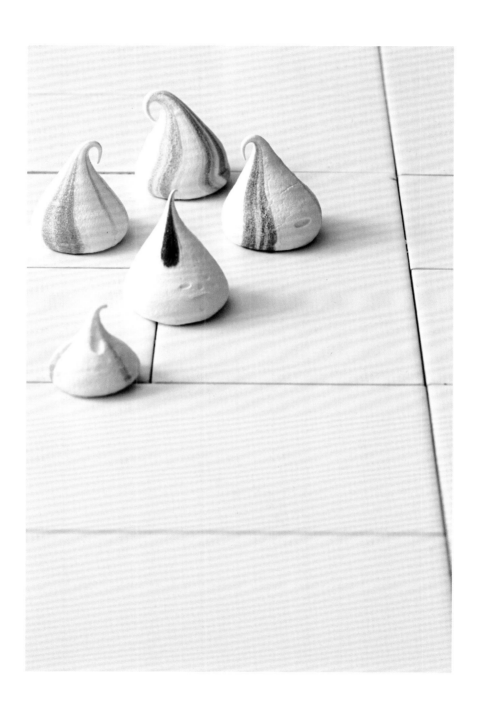

MERINGUE MUSHROOMS

TIMING

PREP approx. 15 mins (with meringue already made)

BAKING 1–2 hours

DECORATING 20 mins

MAKES approx. 15 mushrooms

INGREDIENTS

1 recipe Basic Meringue (page 221)

20 g (¾ oz) Dutch cocoa

100 g (3½ oz) chopped dark chocolate

METHOD

Preheat your oven to 90°C (195°F) and prep two baking trays with pre-cut baking paper.

Fill a piping bag with your meringue (no need for a nozzle), and snip about 4 cm (1½ in) off the point of the piping bag with scissors. Use a small blob of meringue under each corner of your baking paper to stick it to each baking tray. Meringue is super-sticky, and nothing makes me twitch more than when you're trying to pipe meringues and the baking paper keeps pulling up. So this little trick will help the paper stay stuck to the trays.

Pipe random-sized dollops of meringue onto the paper: squeeze your piping bag close to the paper and keep squeezing as you pull up, then release the pressure and keep pulling up to create a little tail. These will be the bases of the mushrooms; pipe about 15 of them.

Pipe the tops onto the second tray: squeeze your piping bag about 1 cm (½ in) off the baking paper, and keep squeezing at that height so the meringue stays flatter and spreads out. Then stop squeezing and flick the piping bag in a semicircle while pulling away at the same time. Dust the tops of your mushroom meringues with a small amount of cocoa before putting them in the oven.

Bake for 1–2 hours; they will be done when the meringues come cleanly away from the baking paper. Remove from the oven and allow to cool.

To decorate, put your dark chocolate in a suitable bowl and melt in the microwave in 20-second bursts, stirring between each burst. When the chocolate is ready, dip each mushroom top in chocolate so just the base is coated, and sit it on top of a mushroom base. Push down slightly so that the pointy tip pushes into the underside of the top—the chocolate will set and secure it in place.

Store in an airtight container for up to 7–10 days.

GIANT MERINGUES

TIMING

PREP approx. 15 mins
(with meringue
already made)

BAKING 2–3 hours

MAKES approx. 3

INGREDIENTS

2 tablespoons
freeze-dried fruit or
Dutch cocoa

1 recipe Basic
Meringue (page 221)

METHOD

Preheat your oven to 100°C (200°F) and prep a baking tray with pre-cut baking paper.

Roughly fold your flavour (fruit or cocoa) through your meringue. If you are using whole or sliced freeze-dried fruit, crush it with your hands so that there are chunks *and* powder.

Use a small blob of meringue under each corner of your baking paper to stick it to the baking tray. Using a large spoon or spatula, scoop large, fist-sized rustic dollops of meringue and drop them onto the tray.

Bake for 2–3 hours; they will be done when the meringues come away cleanly from the baking paper. Remove from the oven and allow to cool.

Store in an airtight container for up to 10 days.

FLAVOUR SUGGESTIONS

The 2 tablespoons of freeze-dried fruit or Dutch cocoa could be replaced with 2 tablespoons of crushed nuts, or a mix of other ingredients you have on hand (how about some leftover crumble from dessert?). Try blueberry & lemon, hazelnut & cocoa, feijoa & crumble, or ground-up pecan praline. The flavours are endless, so be inspired. (If you're using two flavours, go with 1 tablespoon of each.)

OPPOSITE Giant Meringues flavoured with cocoa (front) and with blueberry & lemon (back).

GOURMET S'MORES

TIMING

PREP approx. 15 mins (with ingredients already made)

SETTING approx. 30 mins

MAKES 15 s'mores

INGREDIENTS

1 recipe Vanilla Bean Marshmallows (page 217), uncut

30 Graham Crackers (page 195)

200 g (7 oz) Dark Chocolate Ganache (page 115), ratio 1:2

½ recipe Salted Caramel (page 129)

METHOD

Prepare all of the ingredients as per their individual recipe instructions. Make your ganache fresh before assembly, as you want it to be a runny consistency (i.e. not set).

Cut your marshmallow into square portions 5 x 5 cm (2 x 2 in). Using a food blowtorch, toast the outer edges of each square of marshmallow—be careful to only slightly toast the marshmallow until slightly coloured, or you will either light it on fire and/or melt it to goo, which is premature in the S'more process. Don't be premature in your goo.

Lay out 15 graham crackers, add a dollop of ganache to each cracker and squash a square of marshmallow onto the ganached cracker. Top the marshmallow with more ganache and a dollop of salted caramel, add another cracker to the top and allow to set.

You can either eat them as they are, or put in the microwave for 5 seconds at a time to warm the marshmallow and give an altogether melty gooey delicious experience.

If there are any left over, you can store them in an airtight container in the fridge for up to 2 months.

MALLOW DOMES

TIMING

PREP approx. 4 hours including setting time (or allow marshmallow domes to set overnight)

BAKING approx. 15 mins

MAKES 12 domes

INGREDIENTS

½ recipe Vanilla Bean Marshmallow mixture (page 217)

½ recipe Graham Cracker dough (page 195)

½ recipe Salted Caramel (page 129)

200 g (7 oz) chopped dark chocolate

If I had to describe these to anyone I would say this: one day a s'more met a mallowpuff and fell in love and did sexy stuff, and the mallowpuff got knocked up and their love child was born and they named it Mallow Dome.

METHOD

Before you start, you will need a 6 cm (2½ in) dome mould (I use a silicone one for these), and a round cookie cutter slightly larger than your mould.

Prepare your mould by spraying with cooking spray. Make your marshmallow, then put it in a piping bag and cut off the tip about 2 cm (¾ in) from the end.

Marshmallow is fucken sticky as shit—putting it in a piping bag makes it easier to deal with. Note: as soon as the marshmallow stops whipping it starts to set, so don't fuck around. Get it in the bag and pipe it into the dome moulds straight away. Don't overfill or you will have a wonky dome. You *can* flatten the marshmallow using an offset spatula sprayed with cooking spray, but work fast 'cause it is already setting by this stage.

Allow your domes to set for about 2 hours, or overnight.

Preheat your oven to 160°C (315°F) and prep a baking tray with a piece of baking paper. Make the graham cracker dough as per the recipe, roll it out and use your round cookie cutter to cut circles out of the chilled dough. Transfer the circles to your prepped tray and bake for about 15 mins or until crispy around the edges.

If you don't happen to have caramel lying around, firstly, who are you?! You should *always* have caramel lying around; it should be a fridge staple just like milk and butter. Let's just assume you are new to this caramel-is-life gig, so make a batch of Salted Caramel as per the recipe. Allow it to cool before using.

When you're ready to assemble your mallow domes, put your chocolate in a suitable bowl and melt it in the microwave in bursts of 30 seconds; stir after each burst to distribute the heat. Dip the base of each graham cracker circle in the chocolate, put it on a piece of baking paper and allow the chocolate to set.

Continued overleaf

Once the chocolate is set, lay out your graham cracker circles on a cooling rack with a tray underneath. Put a small dollop of caramel on each graham cracker and place your marshmallow domes flat side down on top of the caramel. Don't use too much caramel, as the domes will slide off the crackers and that is about as annoying as a really annoying thing. Chill your mallow domes for about 30 mins to allow the caramel to adhere the mallow to the cracker.

While your domes are chilling, melt your chocolate again in the microwave. Now pour chocolate over each dome so they are completely covered. Tap your tray on the bench to allow the chocolate to smooth out and any excess to drip down into the tray below.

Using an offset spatula while the chocolate is still soft, move the domes from the cooling rack back onto a piece of baking paper and allow the chocolate to set.

These will keep for about 2 months in an airtight container at room temperature (but let's be honest, you'll have eaten them all well before that).

CHRISTMAS TARTS

TIMING

PREP approx. 1 hour (with fruit mince and dough already made)

BAKING approx. 15 mins

MAKES 15 square tarts

INGREDIENTS

¼ recipe Christmas Fruit Mince (page 139)

1 recipe Shortbread dough (page 183)

For this recipe, you need to make your fruit mince and dough in advance (the fruit mince needs at least 2 weeks to mature!).

METHOD

Preheat your oven to 160°C (315°F). Generously grease your tart tray with cooking spray. I use a square silicone tray 'cause squares are cool, but honestly use whatever tray you find in your kitchen; these are epicly delicious and no one will care if they are squares or circles.

Portion the dough into small scoops. I have a different-sized cookie scoop for every occasion, but just grab whatever you have on hand—the portions will vary depending on the tin you are using, too. Push the dough into the tray using your fingers, or if you have one of those fancy wooden tart formers use that. Just so you know, I don't have a fancy tart former. But last Christmas when Magnolia Kitchen was cranking out the tarts, I had my husband make one for us and it actually works surprisingly well.

Back to pushing the dough with your fingers. Try to get the dough as even around the edges and on the bottom as possible, and make sure you extend it above the top of the tray. Save about 2 portions of dough to add on top of the tarts.

Now add 1 tablespoon of fruit mince to each tart, topping with some rough pieces of saved dough. Bake for about 15 mins, until the tarts colour slightly.

Because these tarts are made with shortbread they are super-buttery and delicate—so chill them in their tin before removing.

If like me you are like, *bleh*, fruit mince, then try the variations overleaf for a less traditional version that will have you impressing anyone that allows one past their lips.

FLAVOUR INSPO FOR CHRISTMAS TARTS

─────

SPICED WHITE CHOCOLATE TARTS
400 g (14 oz) White Chocolate Ganache, ratio 1:2 (page 115)
1½ tablespoons mixed spice
½ teaspoon salt
60 g (2 oz) dried cranberries
60 g (2 oz) shelled pistachios

When you have pressed the dough into the tins, bake the shells without any filling for about 12 mins or until they start to colour slightly. Allow to cool in the tin before removing.

Make the ganache, then stir through the mixed spice and salt. Put the ganache in a piping bag, snip off about 1.5 cm (⅝ in) from the bottom, and squirt ganache into the cooled tarts so it reaches the top of the shells.

Top with cranberries and pistachios and allow the ganache to set.

SPICED DARK CHOCOLATE TARTS
100 g (3½ oz) roasted pecans
400 g (14 oz) Dark Chocolate Ganache, ratio 1:2 (page 115)
2 tablespoons mixed spice
1 teaspoon salt flakes
100 g (3½ oz) Salted Caramel (page 129)

When you have pressed the dough into the tins, bake the shells without any filling for about 12 mins or until they start to colour slightly. Allow to cool in the tin before removing.

Keep 15 whole pecans aside and roughly chop the rest.

Make the ganache and stir through the mixed spice and salt flakes. Put the ganache in a piping bag and snip off about 1.5 cm (⅝ in) from the bottom.

Put a teaspoon of chopped pecans in the bottom of each cooled tart shell and cover with a dollop of salted caramel. Fill each tart with ganache so it reaches the top of the shell. Place a whole roasted pecan on top and allow the ganache to set.

ALLERGY-FRIENDLY STRAWBERRY & NUTMEG ICE CREAM

FREE FROM GLUTEN, EGGS, DAIRY AND ANIMAL PRODUCTS

TIMING

PREP AND CHILLING
4–5 hours

MAKES approx. 1.8 kg (4 lb) ice cream

INGREDIENTS

1 kg (2 lb 4 oz) coconut cream

600 g (1 lb 5 oz) frozen strawberries

200 g (7 oz) maple syrup

½ teaspoon good-quality vanilla bean paste

1 teaspoon vanilla extract

1 tablespoon grated nutmeg

The only reason this recipe exists is that we needed a creative way to photograph the Allergy-friendly Double Chocolate Cookies (page 191). They may be delicious cookies, but they look like black pancakes in photos by themselves— so I decided that allergy-friendly ice cream was the best solution (thanks to wonderful photographer Lottie for the suggestion!). Seriously, though, now that this recipe exists I am left wondering where the fuck it's been all my life!

METHOD

Chill your coconut cream, in its can or carton, in the freezer for about 1 hour prior to starting this recipe—this will make sure the milk and cream separate inside.

DO NOT SHAKE THE COCONUT CREAM. Turn your can/carton upside down to open it, and drain out the liquid. You will be left with solidified coconut cream, which is thick and almost looks like yoghurt. Scoop the thick coconut cream into the bowl of your stand mixer and whisk on high for about 7 mins or until the coconut cream thickens and looks like over-whipped cream.

While the coconut cream is whipping, prepare your strawberries. Roughly chop 200 g (7 oz) of them and set aside. Put the remaining strawberries in a blender along with the maple syrup, vanillas and nutmeg, and blend until combined and the strawberries are puréed.

Add the puréed strawberries to the mixer bowl with the whisked coconut cream and fold together until combined. Add the chopped strawberries and fold to combine. Scrape the ice cream into a freezer-safe bowl or container and freeze for 20 mins. Remove from the freezer and whisk by hand, then put back in the freezer for another 20 mins. Repeat the freezing and whisking until your ice cream is too thick to whisk, then cover and store in the freezer for at least 1 hour before serving.

SWEET TREATS & DRINKS

GOURMET HOT CHOCOLATE

TIMING

PREP 8 mins

SERVES 2

INGREDIENTS

300 g (10½ oz) milk

200 g (7 oz) Dark Chocolate Ganache, ratio 1:1 (page 115)

cocoa for dusting

Vanilla Bean Marshmallows (page 217) to serve

METHOD

Heat the milk in a milk frother (if you don't have one, just heat in a pot on the stove).

Divide the ganache between two mugs, then pour 50 g (1¾ oz) of your hot milk into each mug and give them a good stir. Pour in the remaining hot milk. Top with cocoa and a few marshmallows.

If you're a caffeine fiend, you can add 'instant espresso' coffee* with the first lot of hot milk; we call this a mocha. (Okay okay, I know everyone calls it a mocha when you mix chocolate and coffee.)

*You can buy 'instant espresso' coffee powder and make espresso to your taste by combining 1 teaspoon powder with your preferred amount of hot water.

GOURMET HOT CARAMEL

TIMING

PREP 8 mins

SERVES 1

INGREDIENTS

250 g (9 oz) milk

50 g (1¾ oz) Salted Caramel (page 129)

cocoa for dusting

Vanilla Bean Marshmallows (page 217) to serve

METHOD

Heat your milk in a milk frother—if you don't have one, just heat it on the stove top.

Put the salted caramel in your glass, making sure to liberally dribble it up the sides of the glass. Pour the hot milk into the glass, top with cocoa and a few marshmallows, and enjoy.

If you're a caffeine fiend, then stir 'instant espresso' coffee* into the hot milk just before pouring it in.

*You can buy 'instant espresso' coffee powder and make espresso to your taste by combining 1 teaspoon powder with your preferred amount of hot water.

CASHEW MILK

TIMING

SOAKING 5 hours,
ideally overnight

PREP/MAKING 15 mins

MAKES approx.
1.5 litres (52 fl oz)

INGREDIENTS

400 g (14 oz) raw
cashews

hot water to cover

1.5 kg (3 lb 5 oz) cold
water

½ teaspoon good-
quality vanilla bean
paste

1 teaspoon vanilla
extract

*You can use this as a dairy-free alternative in
EVERYTHING, including coffee, smoothies, baking and
breakfasts. We use our nut milk in-store to make our
Allergy-friendly Salted Caramel Cashew Fudge (page 208),
and we now offer it as one of our dairy-free options for
customers' coffees.*

METHOD

Put your cashews in a bowl and cover with hot water. Cover the bowl and
leave the cashews to soak overnight, or for at least 5 hours.

Once your nuts are soaked, rinse them in fresh water and put in your
blender along with the cold water and vanillas. Blend on high for
5–8 mins.

Place a large sieve over a bowl and line it with muslin cloth. Pour some
of the nut mixture into the muslin. Gather up the sides, and squeeze the
milk through the muslin cloth. This is called milking the nuts. (Look at
the photo and snigger with me ☺)

Once you have got as much milk out of the nuts as you can, empty the
pulp into a container. Repeat this nut-milking process until you have
a bowl filled with milk and a container filled with pulp. Keep the pulp,
as this can be used to make our Allergy-friendly Cookie Sandwiches
(page 193)—this is actually how the cookies came to exist. Waste not,
want not.

Store the milk in a reusable bottle; it will keep in the fridge for 5–7 days.

STRAWBERRY & LEMON SODA SYRUP

TIMING

PREP 10 mins

COOKING 30 mins

MAKES approx. 550 g (1 lb 4 oz)

INGREDIENTS

260 g (9¼ oz) caster sugar

120 g (4¼ oz) lemon juice

150 g (5½ oz) water

100 g (3½ oz) frozen strawberries

1 teaspoon lemon zest

METHOD

Put all the ingredients in a pot and bring to a gentle boil, stirring occasionally.

Once the sugar is dissolved and the strawberries have become pulpy, use a sieve to scoop all of the chunks into a blender and blend on high until not chunky. Put the strawberry purée back into the pot and gently boil for a further 10 mins. Allow to cool, then store in a reusable bottle in the fridge, where it will keep for approximately 4 months.

Add about 30 g (1 oz) to a glass with some ice and top with soda water. Garnish with finely sliced strawberries and lemon if desired.

This syrup can also be mixed with vodka for a summer cocktail, combined with soda and bubbly wine, or added to your favourite punch.

GRAPEFRUIT & GINGER SODA SYRUP

TIMING

PREP 10 mins

COOKING 30 mins

MAKES approx. 550 g (1 lb 4 oz)

INGREDIENTS

260 g (9½ oz) caster sugar

120 g (4¼ oz) grapefruit juice

150 g (5½ oz) water

2 tablespoons honey

1 tablespoon grated fresh ginger

1 teaspoon grapefruit zest

METHOD

Put all the ingredients in a pot and bring to a gentle boil, stirring occasionally, for about 30 mins. Allow to cool, then store in a reusable bottle in the fridge, where it will keep for approximately 4 months.

Add about 30 g (1 oz) to a glass with some ice and top with soda water. Garnish with finely sliced ginger and grapefruit if desired.

This syrup is also super-tasty as a winter warmer—add about 30 g (1 oz) to a mug and top with boiling water.

INDEX

ACKNOWLEDGEMENTS

Yon from Claybird Ceramics was kind enough to custom-make many of the beautiful ceramic pieces you see throughout the book, as well as my infamous gold-drip mugs.

You will notice my finger and neck bling in the photos throughout—all of the pieces are by my good friends and talented ladies Kim from Wicken Jewellery and Del from Love Winter. Huge thanks also to Asrin from Asrin Makeup for making my face look legit.

Victoria from Milsom Bell Ltd collected the most stunning selection of props for the shoot.

Huge thanks to Lottie for her amazing work with the photographs—she is an absolute talent and an inspiration to work with. Many thanks also to Jenny, Leanne and the team at Allen & Unwin, including freelancers Teresa, Kate and Sarah and freelance designer Megan.

Thanks again to my staff a.k.a. the cake fluffers: Charlotte, Sarah, Sam and Abby. If you hadn't realised by now, I love these girls. Magnolia Kitchen, this book and I (in general) would be up shit creek without a paddle if it wasn't for them.